Practical Motorhome & RV Living Start-Up Guide

101 Real- Life Useable Hacks Tips & Tricks for Full-Time RV Living

By

Linda Breakstone

Copyright © 2020 – **Parma Books**

All Rights Reserved.

No part of this publication may be reproduced, stored in a retrieval system or transmitted in any form or by any means, electronic, mechanical, photocopying, recording or otherwise without the proper written consent of the copyright holder, except as permitted under Sections 107 & 108 of the 1976 United States Copyright Act, without the prior written permission of the publisher.

Parma Books publishes its books and guides in a variety of electronic and print formats, Some content that appears in print may not be available in electronic format, and vice versa.

Cover & Book Design by Jennifer Rothschild

Contents

Part 1: All About RVs 13

Life in an RV 14

Knowing RVs 24

    History of the Recreational Vehicle 25

    The Economy of the Recreational Vehicle 27

    The Demographics of Recreational Vehicles 29

    The Whys of Recreational Vehicles 30

Types of RVs 33

    Motorhomes 33

        Class A 34

        Class B 37

        Class C 39

    Towable RVs 42

        Travel Trailers 42

        5th Wheel Trailers 45

        Toy Hauler and Sport Utility RV Trailers 47

        Folding and Tent Trailers 49

Understanding RV Terminology 53

Considerations to Make Before Using an RV 60

    Discarding Most of Your Property 61

    Choosing an RV That is Suitable for You 64

    Where to Set Up Home Base 65

    Living With Kids in an RV 66

    RV Living with Pets 67

    Mail-Forwarding Service 69

    Insurance 71

Part 2: RV Life for Novices 74

10 Common RV Mistakes 75

    Campsite Etiquette 76

    Not Bringing in the Awning 77

    Driving the RV Improperly 77

    Not Leveling the RV 78

    Not Disconnecting Cables 79

    Over Packing 80

    Not Defrosting the Freezer 81

    Forgetting to Doublecheck Everything 82

    Ignoring Small Problems 82

    Not Performing Proper Maintenance 83

RV Checklist 84
    RV Essentials 85
    Emergency Items 86
    Food 88
    Household and Kitchen Items 90
    Clothing and Bedroom Stuff 92
    Toys and Gadgets 94
    Toiletries and Personal items 96
    What to Leave Behind 98
    Documents to Carry 99
        Medical Papers 99
        Documents on Insurance 100
        Vehicle-related Documents 100
        Addresses 101
        Pet Information 102
        Legal Papers 102
    Information on Tech 103
    Information and Guides About Your RV 104
Campsite Etiquette Tips 105
    Observe the Rules 106

- Keep the Neighborhood Tidy 107
- Sewer Connections 107
- Mind Your Pet 108
- Late Arrival 108
- Campfires 109
- Parking the Rig 110
- No Trespassing 111
- Cleaning Your RV 112
- The Golden Rule 114

RV Life Logistics 115
- Small Spaces 115
- Staying Connected 116
- Dumping waste 117
- Finding Places to Camp 118
- Keeping Fit 119
- Doing Laundry 120
- Voting 120
- Money Matters 123

Making Friends 125
- Be the First to Make a Move 126

  Join an RV Club 127

  Attend Campground Events 128

  Social Media 129

RV Glamping 132

  Custom Paint 134

  Toy Hauler Deck 135

  Lighting up Your Space 136

  Using Glamping Decor 137

  Add Cozy Beddings to Your Bed 138

  Control the Temperature 138

  Be Organized 139

Pets 140

  Planning the Ideal Itinerary 142

  Packing the Appropriate Gear 142

  Buckle Up 143

  Be Aware of the Weather 144

  Take Potty Breaks 144

  Be Considerate of Your Neighbors 145

Part 3: 101 RV Hacks 147

Food 148

- Use a Campfire to Cook 149
- Use an Instant Pot 149
- Use a Solar Oven 150
- Use a Pizza Stone 151
- Unusual Storage Ideas 151

Sleeping Hacks 153
- Find a Secluded Spot 153
- Turn off the lights at night 154
- Acquire a Good Mattress 155
- Get Comfy Bedding 155
- Limit Screentime 156
- Zippered Bedding 156
- Limit Caffeine 156
- Sleeping Bags Lined with a Sheet 157
- Stick to a Schedule 157

Cleaning and Organizing Hacks 158
- Decrease Your List of Cleaners 158
- Work Smart Not Hard 158
- Cleaning Entry Area 159
- Take a Few Minutes a Day 159

Be Organized ... 159

Use Cleaning Tools that are Space Efficient ... 160

Use Wet Wipes ... 160

Air Freshness is Key ... 160

Use Organizers from Surprising Places. ... 161

Maintenance Hacks ... 162

Cover Up ... 162

Generator Maintenance ... 162

Check Things Out ... 163

Vent it Out ... 163

Lubricate ... 164

Tire Time ... 165

Keep Records ... 165

Fuel ... 166

Lighting ... 166

Staying Healthy ... 168

Dieting ... 168

Shop Often ... 169

Pack a Picnic ... 169

Dine Out One Day ... 169

- Hit the Gym 170
- Get a Gym Membership 170
- Be Active 171
- Plan Meals 171
- Travel Slowly 171
- Water, Water, Water 172

Money 173
- Saving Money 173
  - Travel Seasonally 173
  - Boondock 173
  - Cook More 174
  - Join RV Clubs 174
- Making Money 174
  - Work Online 175
  - Try Workamping 175
  - Find Local Jobs 176
  - Sell Your Services 176
  - Sell Stuff 176
  - Be a Blogger 177

Navigation 178

Practice 178

Observe the Weather 179

Adjust Your Mirrors 179

Don't Drive Tired 179

Go Slow 180

Observe Courtesy 180

Tail Swing is Everything 180

Avoid Tailgating 181

Braking Habits 181

Far Right 181

Safety 182

First Aid 182

Be Defensive 183

Have a Plan 183

Travel in Groups 184

Carry a Smartphone 184

Switch Off the Generator 184

Do Safety Checks 184

Have a Dog 185

Be Diligent 185

Comfort Hacks 186
    Prepare Early 186
    Use Folder Boxes 186
    Install Push Lights 187
    Get Hooked 188
    Get Cushioned 188
    Get What You Pay For 188
    Be Creative 189
    Hanging Storage Everywhere 189
    Regulate Windows 189
Recreation Hacks 190
Conclusion 192

Part 1: All About RVs

Life in an RV

It has always been my life dream to go on a road trip across the United States.

I have always been a lover of nature since I was young. My parents noticed that and would often take me out for nature walks. I loved climbing mountains, swimming in rivers, and exploring the ravines. As I grew older, I became more intrigued by the regional differences in the country. The U.S. is enormous. Most foreign tourists usually forget this fact. A lot of American citizens do not even recognize how enormous their country is. I have always desired to go out and experience all that nature in different regions has to offer.

Despite my dream to travel across the U.S., it took quite a while for it to be practical. I came from a poor background with parents who did not have money to make it possible. They saw my passion, but could only afford to take me on nature walks around our town.

As a young adult, I still could not afford to travel. The little I earned went into paying deep debts that I had. I could not even find the time. There was a lot of work to do. Plus, my friends had no interest in driving across the country for weeks on end. They also had their own financial issues to deal with. I thank God, though, I married a man who also had a love for nature and a dream to travel all over. That love is actually what drew us close together before we got married.

In my forties, however, a unique set of events happened and made my dream of a road trip able to come to reality. With my kids in colleges in different states, my husband and I had the best opportunity to drive all over the country.

At the beginning of 2015, we made the decision to get an RV and travel across the U.S. full time. We have taken years on the road. It feels like we started this adventure just the other day. I can barely remember my life before this journey.

We have experienced a lot of fun times and challenges living in an RV, but I have never enjoyed anything else as much as I enjoy this journey. Well, besides being a mom to two beautiful babies. There has also been a great transformation for both my husband and I since we began our journey. We have even grown closer over the years while traveling full-time.

We have noticed the changes in us with every passing year. However, we recently verified this when we paid one of our kids a visit. We had not visited him for quite a while. When we met, he was amazed and kept saying how much we have changed. He even joined us on a road trip when he was on a school break. He was so curious to experience what we had and see how we had changed. That visit really helped us notice the changes that had taken place, and we recognized it that the experience we had on the road that made it happen.

When someone lives in an RV, he or she adopts new habits. There is just no room for collecting things. We began cutting down on our accumulation of stuff while preparing for our life in an RV. However, when we got in the RV and started our journey, lacking extra space for storage really helped reduce any single remedy we had employed. We have less impulse to go shopping and are no longer bombarded by messages from commercials to buy products since we no longer watch TV as much as we used to. For that reason, we have fewer things and usually purchase only what we need. These days, we focus more on making memories and enjoying sunsets.

In addition, we enjoy partaking in stopovers, hiking, sitting with friends around campfires, exploring nature around us, and just hanging out with new people we have met. We find our pleasure in what we find wherever we are and the company that we have at that moment. We feel comfortable with what we see in a day and do not spend money getting into theme parks.

While we are not that crazy about planning ahead, my husband, Tony, was so excited and did a general plan of the places we were going to visit and what we were likely to see in that area. That plan really came in handy when planning for a visit to certain places like the Florida Keys. However, after a year of traveling, we reduced the number of times we made specific reservations. We began to be loose with our plans and went with the day's happenings. This enabled us to visit different awesome places, make new friends, and evade unfavorable weather.

We began to be laid back since then. I can attest to the fact that I have never been more laid back in my life. For instance, my husband would not have entertained going to Mexico for a doctor's visit four years ago. At the moment, we are so used to going there. I also do not get stressed when something gets lost or breaks. We just plan to purchase a new one or fix the broken one. We usually adapt and move on.

Before we started our journey, we had very few friends and were more introverts. Living in an RV, however, has changed us to more social people than we have ever been. We normally look forward to RV meet-ups, where we have been making lots of friends. We have made quick connections that have remained deep over the years.

Never before have we felt such a strong sense of community while living in a set-up location. We have friends that we digitally keep tabs on frequently. When close to each other, we usually ensure that we meet up with our friends and share stories of our adventures. Sometimes, we plan get-togethers during spring and try our best to attend the campers' meet-ups. At the moment, we have more friends than ever before.

I can talk so much about why I cherish our life on the road. The travel has been epic, and with the opportunities that we have had, we could never have thought about them before our road trip.

We can now visit our friends and family more often and park near their residence. We no longer spend money flying across the country and booking hotels. We visit them like we are just neighbors. With limited travel time, you never get to see the people you love often. You may take even years before visiting them. But, with an RV, we have been able to visit them all and are planning on visiting them again.

We are also not stuck to a holiday timeline. This has become our life, and we are not on a vacay. So, we even out our days with work and play, rather than taking off for a week and jamming the vacation days with lots of sightseeing. We decide on what we wish to see and do not feel entitled to get our money's worth.

Depending on what we wish to explore in the region, we may visit the area for a few days or even weeks. When at the place, we carry on with our normal lives like the locals in the area. We eat at the local restaurants, shop at the local stores, and engage in everyday life. While we are not true citizens of the towns, we usually get a sense of place better than we would on vacation.

Another fun thing we have been doing is boondocking and camping around the fire. It was not our habit to boondock at first, but once we began, we could not get enough of the good times we had. We got to see a lot of possibilities that made us fall deeper in love with this life. We could go to different places and have fun, but camping among the Sedona red rocks is such an epic experience. It was much more fun with friends around. We usually camp in such places as much as we can and get a break from the campgrounds. It is also free, so nothing can beat that.

Things have not been totally smooth, though. We have actually experienced some very hard times. Life in an RV is not as perfect and rosy as it sounds. It's just that the challenges are not so awful that they are worth calling out. Our latest laid back attitude could be contributing to that.

Also, knowing things to do with an RV like dumping the black tanks have gradually become a part of our life. The challenges are not as bad. With time, we got to adapt to life in the RV and got more settled with time.

When we began our journey, it was a bit of a challenge to get the RV serviced. This is essentially due to the fact that the RV is now our home and office. It can be a bit troublesome to have it serviced as we may need to be out of it when the work is being done.

Leaving the RV while it is being serviced would mean finding another place to work or wait as we do other things. During waiting for the RV maintenance, we have had to rent a hotel room, go to a friend's house, or just wait at the service center when we do not want to go far. We once spent the night at a service center. It was not the most scenic of locations, but it was not that bad.

While there are things we can do ourselves, we do not have the whole mechanic toolbox for the problems that arise. We once attempted to install sway bars while in an awkward place. After a couple of parts, we had taken out of the RV broke, and others went missing, we were forced to put the RV back together and find a service shop for it to be fixed.

Driving around big cities is another big challenge we deal with. Before we began the journey, we lived and worked in a city. We would drive to and from work and easily to perform our activities in the city. I would even use public transport once in a while.

Moving about in a car is not so hard, but driving an RV around a city is a totally different case. Most people have no idea how long an RV takes to stop; thus, they keep zipping around you. It can be a bit stressful sometimes. To deal with this, we now try our best to dodge rush hour and take alternative routes.

Booking holiday weekends has also been a challenge, as whiny as it sounds. Now, holidays on weekends usually blend into the calendar, making it hard to remember to plan for it. By luck, we have had holidays booked by chance, spent some holidays boondocking or exploring nature, but sometimes we forget to plan for holidays.

We are not the only ones finding this a challenge. Our friends have also forgotten to plan for holidays occasionally. To reserve space at a campground on Memorial Day weekend, you need to book months before. But, we do not keep such things in mind anymore. I think we should start setting reminders.

So, you may be thinking, "Do these guys have any plans of going on a cruise ship or purchasing some land, or they will keep driving forever?"

Well, I can whole-heartedly state that we plan on being on the road for a much longer time. My husband and I love the life we are having in our RV and what we have gained from this journey. We plan on getting deep into this life and broadening our careers while still in the RV. We are so excited about the future and have big plans.

But before then, I cannot wait to share how much I have learned from this journey and RVs in general. It is my wish that more people get to explore this great country and have their lives changed as we have. I desire that you see the possibility of traveling all over and enjoying nature.

So, dig in and find out more about RV living.

Knowing RVs

The recreational vehicle (RV) is simply a trailer or motor vehicle that has living sections intended for accommodation. There are all sorts of RVs like camper trailers, motorhomes, travel trailers, and campervans, among many more.

Common facilities in an RV are one sleeping facility or more, a kitchen, and a bathroom. These vehicles can vary from the luxurious ones, with things like televisions, air conditioning (AC), quartz countertops, satellite receptors, and water heaters, to the utilitarian vehicles with basic facilities for cooking and sleeping quarters only.

RVs can be either self-motorized or trailers, which are pulled behind a motor vehicle. Most RVs in the market are single-deck. However, it is possible to find a double-deck RV. Most large RVs usually have sides that are expandable. These sides are known as canopies or slide-outs and make it possible for the RV to be more compact in size while on transit.

History of the Recreational Vehicle

In the early days of RVs, the first kind of safari was done in a covered wagon drawn by horses. From circa 1745, this caravan played a vital role in introducing settlers to the interior parts of North America. By the 1920s, the US saw the rise of the modern RV. Clubs meant for RV camping were also set across the country, notwithstanding the camping facilities being limited and the unpaved roads.

Various firms started making house trailers, which at the time were known as trailer coaches. One of the companies that made these trailers at the time is Airstream. The RV industry was highly linked to the mobile home industry until the 1950s.

This is because a lot of mobile homes were shorter than 30 ft, making them easy to transport. In the 1950s, the mobile home and RV industries were separated. RV companies started manufacturing motorhomes that were self-contained.

In Europe, wagons developed for accommodation, instead of transporting goods and people only were made around 1810 in France.

From the 1820s, circus performers and showmen in Britain made good use of them. In 1850, the people in Romani also began living in caravans circa, which they called Vardos.

The earliest motorhomes in Canada were made from around 1910 on bodies of trucks or cars. In 1929, Australia got the earliest recognized motorhome. The motorhome is known for holding the first mobile caravan in Australia. You can find it displayed at the Goolwa museum in Australia.

The Economy of the Recreational Vehicle

The RV industry has such a great impact on the economy. It makes an annual revenue of around $50 billion in the U.S. alone. A lot of businesses (around 23,000) are dealing in the industry at the moment. These businesses are generating approximately 40,000-45,000 primary job opportunities and direct wages of about $3 billion. This is according to the Recreational Vehicle Industry Association (RVIA)

There was a celebration in 2017 by the RV industry to mark its eighth year of growth in sales. According to the

RVIA, the recreational vehicle industry had experienced a growth of more than 200% in those eight years. This growth was, however, expected to decline slightly in 2019 and return with high sales records in 2020.

Apart from the U.S, the RV industry has affected other countries as well. For instance, the RV industry in Canada has made over an annual income of about $7 billion from retail sales. This is according to Statista.

Contrary to Canada, almost $18 billion is made by the RV industry from retail sales. This is because of half a million-plus of RV wholesale shipment.

In 2017, retail locations selling RVs generated indirect loans of about 200,000. These loans amounted to about $8.4 billion from families buying RVs. According to the RVIA, households would purchase an RV for over $45,000, making up the 200,000 loans.

It is possible to find an affordable RV going for less than $10,000 these days. However, average RVs cost much more than that. For instance, Class C and Class B recreational vehicles cost about $100,000 to $150,000, which is much higher than $10,000. Class A motorhomes, on the other hand, cost about $500,000.

According to the Department of Commerce, the exports in the RV industry bring in about $1 billion every year. It generally contributes an annual revenue to the U.S economy of about $6 billion. This is generated from taxes paid.

The Demographics of Recreational Vehicles

So far, Americans make up the largest market share in the RV industry. RV use in the U.S is very much accepted, with forty million people going camping in RVs. They do car-based camping and backyard camping as well.

Millennials are getting used to RV camping; thus, they are about 38% of the 40 million people using RVs. This is despite them making up about 31% of the whole population as per figures derived in 2017. Despite this use of RVs by millennials, Baby Boomers and Gen X make up a substantial segment in the industry, with families between the ages of 35-55 purchasing RVs more in the U.S. According to Statista, campers under the age of 25 make up an approximate of 25% in the U.S.

While young people are gradually enjoying traveling in RVs, the average owner of an RV in the U.S is 45-50 years old. This is according to studies done by the University of Michigan.

So far, about 8 million households in the U.S own an RV. In addition, you can find about 15,000 parking facilities and campgrounds all over the country. These facilities and campgrounds can be either private or public.

The industry has seen a household ownership growth of about 16% growth since 2001. This is in the U.S alone. Compared to the 1980s, households that have owned RVs have grown by about 60%.

Families that own an RV typically earn about $62,000. These households usually use their RVs for at least one month every year.

When it comes to pets, about 55% of RV owners travel around with their pets. This is because most RVs are designed well for traveling with pets.

The Whys of Recreational Vehicles

People buy RVs mainly because they can travel around and go camping as a family. This is much better and easier than the traditional options for camping. Most RV owners state this as the main reason why they bought an RV.

RVs also help in saving costs. That is why they are very popular in North America. Over the traditional vacation at hotels, BnBs, or other kinds of accommodation, a vacation in an RV can cut down on costs by around 60%. A lot of people have said that they fancy RV camping where they can take a walk or hike.

Every year, the ordinary RV owner drives around 4,500 miles. This is according to the University of Michigan. A lot of RV owners have admitted to taking at least three trips around the country in their trailer or vehicle. This is topping up to the common annual vacay.

RV owners have also admitted to taking advantage of some camping locations in the country and enjoy engaging in activities such as boondocking.

The most common destination for RV campers in the U.S is Yosemite National Park. Every single year, the park welcomes over 250,000 campers who have their recreational vehicle.

With time, a lot of people are embracing the RV lifestyle and selling most of their property to start that journey. According to the University of Michigan, about 500,000 RV owners have admitted to using their RVs as their chief places of residence. However, one million Americans usually live in RVs full time, according to research by the Recreation Vehicle Industry Association.

Types of RVs

When trying to decide on the most suitable RV for you, you can find it quite overwhelming as there are many options available in the market. For it to be less overwhelming, it is good to do extensive research, consider your budget, and have a good plan for the places that you would like to travel to. It is also very important that you consider who you will be traveling with.

Here, I will give you a few examples of the kinds of RVs and motorhomes on the market, as well as tell you a few of their advantages and disadvantages. This is going to make it easy for you to make a well-informed decision on the kind of RV that is most suitable for you and your family.

Motorhomes

RV camping can be quite enjoyable and fun for many people. However, different people have different needs. For this reason, it is vital that someone chooses a vehicle that serves their needs best.

An individual must also consider their budget before purchasing an RV. Motorhomes are slightly different from the travel trailer kinds of RVs and have several advantages over them. Normally, they are entirely self-contained, more manageable to set up at campgrounds, and provide more room for the travelers to walk around as you drive.

In the market, you will find three kinds of motorhomes. These three motorhomes have pros and cons as we are about to see.

Class A

These are the largest and most expensive RVs you can find on the market. Dedicated travelers prefer them over other kinds of RVs. Alternatives incorporate purpose-built models as well as converted buses. Their drivelines can be installed up as a puller configuration or a pusher. They are normally powered by gasoline engines or diesel. No special CDL license is needed to run one legally, although some could be as long as 45 feet.

With these motorhomes, you can enjoy many available features as well as the most interior space. You can find some with sections for slide-outs, which expand the living space. Also, most have a master bedroom suite. With a Class A RV, you can get endless appliances and facilities like ice makers, good home entertainment systems, washing machines, as well as bath and shower amenities.

You can also find a lot of storage space for your luggage in the "basement." You can stock your RV with enough stuff that you will need when traveling.

While these Class A RVs are an awesome option for camping and getaways on weekends, their size is very intimidating for a lot of people and are also very expensive. With a Class A recreational vehicle, you will find it challenging to pass through some narrow roads. It may be quite a challenge to park in limited camping sites as well as maneuver the vehicle over a twisty mountain pass.

You may also find it difficult to set up once you arrive at the campsite, or even leave it somewhere to attend to simple errands.

This is why a lot of people prefer to tow along another smaller vehicle to ease the challenge. In addition, the cost of insurance, fuel, and repairs of these RVs are also high compared to other motorhomes, topping up to the initial expensive cost of purchase.

So, if you do not mind towing another car when traveling about, are not intimidated by its size, and have the money, then this is the vehicle for you. With it, you can be sure of plenty of interior space for living, a lot of storage space for your luggage, as well as loads of luxurious amenities.

While they may be unrealistic and unattainable for a lot of people, they are the most suitable option for travelers planning to be on the road for a long time. Retirees and those interested in being full-time travelers love this option. They purchase them often and use them to travel all over.

Class B

Often referred to as camper vans, Class B RVs include a lot of the small-sized vehicles that can hardly be recognized as motorhomes. They are usually created on a conventional full-sized van frame and have a raised roof to facilitate upright walking.

These RVs vary in their motor power as some are powered by gasoline and others by diesel, just like the Class A recreational vehicles.

The Class B travel camper usually offers their purchasers sleeping quarters that are comfortable and all the necessary amenities that they may need. Because of their small size, it is easy for the user to drive and maneuver around in it as well as find parking.

As a user, you can also use the camper van to run your errands or go on a quick road trip. They are fully self-contained and can conveniently accommodate a couple of travelers. Campers using Class B RVs usually appreciate access to air conditioning and heating, hot water, a refrigerator, showers, sink, and toilets. While they are usually a bit expensive to purchase, they are much more pocket-friendly when it comes to their operation.

These RVs' interior space is normally a bit cramped up. Things can be very uncomfortable for you if there are more than two people in the RV. The appliances in the camper van are also a lot smaller than the usual appliances.

Luxuries like a full-sized entertainment system or laundry facility are usually not included because of the size of the van. Also, you cannot carry many things because the capacity of the cargo area is also small.

So, for people who want a manageable campsite vehicle that is easy to maneuver around in and costs less to maintain and fuel, the Class B RV is the most suitable for them. They will find it very convenient and probably use it to run their errands.

Besides the limited space and amenities, the camper vans are very good and economical. You can take a trip with one of your friends, your spouse, or family and enjoy it.

Because of its convenience and pocket-friendly nature, people traveling alone or with one other person usually find these vehicles very beneficial.

People who are still working normally use it occasionally for quick road trips over the weekend or holidays.

Class C

These RVs are neither large nor small. They are midsized and vary from 20 to 33 feet. They are constructed on existing van and truck bodies when being made. Large families and groups going on a limited budget road trip often use these recreational vehicles. While they are cheaper to purchase, these vehicles offer a lot of benefits that are similar to Class A recreational vehicles.

With these vehicles, you can enjoy more space than in Class B RVs and a lot of the same facilities as in a Class A as you live with your loved ones during the road trip. Normally, you will find a lot of sleeping space, a good kitchen, as well as shower and toilet facilities. You can also come across models that are larger and have a master bedroom suite in the back. Others forgo this alternative and go for a profile that is easy to maneuver around in.

In these RVs, tables, and couches can be converted to beds. Also, the compartment hanging above the automobile can be utilized as an additional sleeping space or for storage. Because of the vehicle's compartmental layout, gaining access to the vehicle is easy through the doors on the side.

Although they are great and spacious, Class C recreational vehicles can be very challenging to maneuver around in, just like Class A RVs. They are a bit easy to handle in confined campsites.

Most travelers usually have a separate towable vehicle for outings and running errands. When it comes to insurance, costs of fuel and general maintenance, these vehicles are somewhat better than Class A RVs. Nonetheless, they are still a bit more costly than Class B vehicles.

So, if you are looking forward to taking a road trip together with your whole family, this would be the best vehicle for you. In it, you can enjoy the extra sleeping and storage space, as well as the basic amenities in the vehicle. Remember, it will also cut down your maintenance and fuel costs.

While you may find it a bit challenging to drive and may have to tow another vehicle behind it, the vehicle remains as one of the best vehicles for family road trips.

You can travel on a limited budget with your spouse and kids and enjoy the basic feature of RV trips as well as camping.

Towable RVs

When deciding on the kind of RV that is most suitable for you, it is vital that you carefully weigh its aptitudes and values with your requirements and intentions.

When it comes to RVs, towable RVs offer much more advantage over full-sized RVs. Initially, they are less expensive, more authentic, and also present the advantage of a detachable vehicle, which can be used to run errands and explore different places.

There are different types of towable RVs:

Travel Trailers

These are large portable containers filled with living spaces and all of the conveniences of home.

They are constructed on top of a standard trailer frame and are equipped with a number of amenities. These trailers can be luxurious or be kept simple; it all depends on the one that you purchase.

Their features include kitchens, small refrigerators, bathrooms, and their own water supplies. These trailers vary in size, with some that are equipped with parts that open up to give campers more space inside to stretch out.

The travel trailer RVs usually connect to standard ball hitch receivers, thus giving them a wide variety of towing vehicles that can be utilized.

Any truck or SUV rated to handle the weight can pull these trailers. For this reason, you do not have to buy another vehicle to cater to any distinct necessities.

While they are very beneficial, these trailers can be a bit tricky to maneuver. It may also be a big challenge to reverse the vehicle when the trailer is attached.

People with living quarters that are extended in the rear usually face a big challenge when maneuvering down the road.

These trailers can also pose a problem as they require leveling when parked.

The setting and removal of the vehicle towing the trailer can also be a challenge.

If you already have a vehicle that you can use to tow a trailer and also use to run your errands, you might want to consider purchasing this trailer.

However, be cautious about extreme tail swing, reversing the vehicle, as well as driving in confined and cramped areas.

A travel trailer is good for full-time travelers as well as small families with a desire to go on a road trip. It all depends on your budget.

5th Wheel Trailers

These trailers are pretty much like their smaller travel trailer counterparts, but with only one major difference. 5th wheel trailers usually have a gooseneck connector, which is attached to the tow vehicle. This set up has both advantages and disadvantages.

The gooseneck stretches out the rear of the towing truck and attaches from the base of an overhanging part of the trailer, thus making the towing of the vehicle simpler. The truck is then able to maneuver well as there is more support from the core of the truck.

Because of the overhanging part of the trailer, there is also extra space inside the trailer that you cannot find in a regular pull-behind travel trailer. The connections are much more powerful and more comfortable to operate than general ball hitches.

The one challenge about these trailers is that you have to have some specific type of vehicle for you to tow them. A truck with a flat or open bed is compulsory.

Large families may find this challenging because of the limited space. Living in a truck cab while in restricted areas may also be challenging for the trailer owner.

The law also forbids one from riding in a vehicle that is being towed. In comparison to SUVs or commuter vans, exploring places all over may be less pleasant to the user.

With the advantages of the gooseneck rig and the many modern facilities and luxuries, this may be the right vehicle for you. However, do not forget that the towing vehicle ought to be a specific kind of vehicle.

The cost, flexibility, and dependability of these characteristics make these trailers a favorite of a lot of recreational vehicle fans.

Toy Hauler and Sport Utility RV Trailers

These trailers have features that are a combination of the sport-utility trailer and the travel RV trailer. Anyone wishing to carry along their snowmobiles, ATVs, and dirt bikes when going for a road trip would love these trailers.

One great thing about them is that they have a compartment that is meant for keeping sports vehicles in the rear, making it suitable for people who would love to carry their sports vehicles to camp. They also have a wall that becomes a loading ramp. This wall folds up and provides space when needed. The compartments at the front are the spaces where campers can live in.

These trailers are for fans of spending time outdoors who wish to play around with motorsports while out on camping rips. Like the more expensive trailers, the toy haulers have features that campers enjoy. Campers have some extra space for their small motor cars, gear, and tools.

Like every other recreational vehicle, these have a disadvantage as well. In the toy hauler, the living quarters inside the trailer is limited. Only a small part of the space inside is advantageous for campers.

This also poses a challenge as some people do not like being close to motor-driven machines and equipment. There may be an unpleasant odor of chemicals like fuel, oil, and many more. These chemicals may pose an environmental risk to the users of the trailer.

If you love and engage in motorsports and would wish to carry your motor toys with you to camping, then this is for you. You should, however, be cautious of the hazards it may pose to you and the people you are traveling with.

With a sport utility RV, you can go out with your friends and enjoy time engaging in motorsports together. You will also enjoy the basic things that ensure campers' comfort and proper resting amid adventures.

Folding and Tent Trailers

Of all the towable trailers you can find on the market, this is one of the smallest of the towable RVs. In these RVs, you will find parts that are collapsible hence decreasing their outer profiles and making them comfortable to store when not being utilized. These RVs are made different, with some made with hard composite surfaces that collapse down and others made of long-lasting tent canvas.

For people who enjoy going on camping adventures occasionally, these trailers are a good option for them. They are easy to move about with and are lightweight.

You can also get a lot of options for towing vehicles. Vehicles equipped with proper ball hitch receivers like full-sized sedans, station wagons, and small trucks, can be used to pull any of these RVs. Like other RVs, the folding and tent trailer usually provide the campers with the simple essentials needed for survival, making the overall camping experience much more pleasant.

However, it is difficult to carry extra stuff with you because of the way these trailers are designed. As a user, you may find it tricky to carry a lot of things in them. Any equipment and supplies that you have must be carried separately.

Also, the joints where the walls fold and the canvas parts are likely to wear out and eventually have leaks, hence making life for the camper a bit challenging. In these RVs, you will find minimal basic essentials, such as kitchen equipment and toilets. In some models, these facilities may be totally absent.

These trailers are very affordable and are easy to move about in. If you are an occasional camper with a vehicle you can tow it with, you can opt for this version.

When using it, keep in mind that the space inside is limited, so you cannot go around with a lot of people or store much in the vehicle. Keep checking the folding hinges for any failure that may occur. Failure of hinges may expose you to the weather that may make camping uncomfortable.

These RVs are especially great for camping beginners since they are excellent part-time camping vehicles.

Hopefully, by now, you have a rough idea of the kind of RV that would suit your needs. You can have either a fully motorized and luxurious motorhome or a towable RV trailer as they are all unique and diverse in shape, class, style, and size.

All of them have their advantages and disadvantages that you should be familiar with before purchase. When it comes to deciding which vehicle shall be your close friend when exploring the country, it is up to you to make the right decision.

Understanding RV Terminology

As a newbie in this awesome and adventurous world, you will realize that there are certain slang words that RV campers use when interacting with each other. Sometimes, even a camper who has been on the journey for years may find a new slang word that they have never heard or used before. However, experienced RV campers may take a wild guess and get the meaning of the word right.

So what are these words, and what are their meanings?

Below are some general phrases and words used in the RV world that can help you when purchasing an RV. These words will also help you when interacting with fellow RV owners, as well as speaking about your RV issues to your insurance company.

With knowledge of this lingo, you may influence people into thinking that you are an experienced, full-time RV camper, even if you are a beginner. I hope this will help you in talking to other people in the RV world.

Basement – This is the area used for storage. This area is under your motorhome's main area and is accessed from outside. These areas are normally in class A or Class C motorhomes.

Chucking - This is a back and forth movement that is usually violent. It is encountered when towing and normally generated if the trailer is unbalanced or moving on a bumpy road.

Toad (Dinghy) – This term describes the vehicle being towed by your motorhome.

Coach - This is another name for the Class A RV.

Chassis – This stands for the frame that holds the entire RV.

Extended Stay Site - this is the campsite where campers stay for a long time. Some stay in these camps for months and others for a whole season.

Black Water Tank – This is the place where the wastewater in the RV is held.

Blue Boy - These are wheeled plastic totes that are portable. They are normally used to move the waste tank sewage from the trailer to the dumpsite. It is normally towed by the tow vehicle at a very slow speed.

Boondocking / Dry camping – Also known as "roughing it," boondocking is camping without any external hookups or resources, like electricity, sewer, and water.

Fiver – This is another name for a 5th wheel RV.

Dump Station – This is the place where the black and grey tanks are emptied.

Fresh Water Tank – This is where drinking water is kept.

Cockpit – This is the driver's seat at the motorhome, the spot where he or she drives from.

Dually – This is a tow vehicle that is light-duty or a pickup truck. Its rear axle usually has four tires.

Full Hookup- This is a campsite with all the resources needed, like sewage, water, and electricity.

Full-Timers – These are campers that live the RV lifestyle throughout the year.

Batwing - This is the name used for the TV antenna in standard RVs. These antennas resemble a pair of wings.

Holding Tanks – This describes the three distinct water tanks that most motorhomes have. These are the fresh, grey, and black tanks.

Galley - This is the other name for the kitchen.

Hula Skirt – This is a skirt that is installed at a motorhome's back bumper. It is important as it helps stop trash that is discharged from the rear wheels from causing damage to the vehicles following the motorhome.

Gray Water Tank – This is the place where water used from showers and sinks is deposited.

King Pin - This is a piece of a round-shaped cylinder that usually hangs down at the front of a 5th wheel trailer. This piece attaches to the clamps of the 5th wheel block at the rear of the tow vehicle.

Newbie - This is someone new to the trailer world

Hose Bib - A campsite tap with clean water.

Part-Timers – These are people who still have a permanent place of residence, but live a few months of the year in their RV.

Honey Wagon - A trailer or truck with a big liquid tank on top of it. This tank usually goes around places pumping out the waste tanks on RVs.

Jake Brake - This is the engine brake which is used on some diesel-powered vehicles.

Puller – This is a Class A Diesel RV with a diesel motor placed at the front.

Sani-Dump - This is the other name for a sewer dump station. It is where campers empty their trash tanks.

Slideout – This is an RV feature that opens up to generate more space for living. It is normally found in the bedroom and living rooms.

Snowbirds – These are people who love to go south with their RVs during wintertime. During the summer, they usually go north.

Sticks N Bricks - This is the name for a regular kind of permanent home.

Stinky Slinky- This is what is also known as the flexible sewer hose. It is used to drain the waste tanks of the RV.

Genset - This is the electric generator used in most motorhomes.

Reefer - This refers to the electric refrigerator or the LP gas.

Tail Swing - This term is used to describe the additional distance at the RV's rear end, which is used when making a turn. When the space between the RV end and the rear wheel is longer, the tail swing will also be larger. When turning corners in a cramped location, it is vital that you have an idea of the state of your tail swing.

Pusher – These are Class A diesel-powered RVs that have the diesel motor positioned at the rear.

Triple Tow - This is the courageous act of towing your RV plus an extra trailer behind it — for instance, an RV and a boat.

Pull-Through – This is a campsite with ample entrance and exit that make it possible for campers to set up and move on without always having to line up.

Rig – This is another name for a motorhome.

Wheel Chocks - These are slanted blocks, which are normally manufactured from plastic materials. They can also sometimes be made from wood. They keep the RV from rolling.

Workamping - This is the name used to describe campers who do work free work at campsites and the benefits they receive. They are sometimes paid a small wage. This is something that full-timers do to cut down on living costs.

Tow Dolly - This is a two-wheeled trailer that is small in size. They are used for attaching a tow vehicle to the rear end of an RV.

Wally Dock - This is a term used by seasoned RV users to describe overnight parking of your RV at Walmart

Considerations to Make Before Using an RV

So, the fact that you have come this far into the book could mean that you are thinking of moving into an RV. If so, there are a number of fundamental things that you should understand prior to making that great step from living your normal life to living in an RV.

There are things you need to do broad research about to decide on whether changing to the mobile way of life will be propitious for you. Moving into an RV is not an easy thing for some people. Some people take the matter with a lot of seriousness. Others, however, consider it to be a great mistake that they would not dare do.

Could be you are like I was, dreaming of a life on the road exploring all sorts of places? You do not mind living in an RV for a whole year or more. However, before you start this commitment, it is necessary that you recognize that this step will be life-changing in so many ways. You will not always enjoy things as each day has its own good and bad times.

For this reason, you ought to do extensive research before you buy any RV. With the necessary knowledge, you will be able to decide on whether leaving a comfortable home for a life in an automobile is the best choice to make.

So, before you move out into your RV, below are some things that you should keep in mind:

Discarding Most of Your Property

Before getting into the RV lifestyle, you need to make a decision on which is more valuable to you – your property or your passion to live a more simplistic and less troublesome life. A lot of people who choose to be full-timers usually sell their homes and everything apart from one of the vehicles. This is the vehicle that they use to tow their travel unit.

To free up lots of space, most of these campers usually discard their artwork, furniture, and other things that occupy space. When choosing this lifestyle, you must consider the little things you loved like:

- Books

- Large electronics

- Extra clothing

- Hobby materials

- Pets

- Collectables

- Magazines

- Holiday decorations

- Bulky electronic appliances

- Cases of family photos

- Most of your furniture

As a newbie RVer, you must consider that there are very many things that you will need to do away with. For that reason, think hard about the decisions you make.

Discarding property is not easy for everyone. Some people find it very challenging to make this change. So, instead of getting rid of their property, they usually rent some storage units where they can put their belongings. After that, they travel for months without worrying about their property.

Also, there are those who are lucky enough to have friends or family with ample storage space for their belongings at their homes. They usually buy storage sheds then go on to their trip. Over time, the sheds have proven to be less expensive than the rented units. They are much safer and easy to keep tabs on your property. When you buy a shed, the amount of money you will have spent to purchase the shed will be recovered in a year. In case you decide to go back to your normal life or embrace a full-time RV lifestyle, you can sell the shed and make some money from it.

People normally store items so as a way to feel secure. It also helps them make a good comeback from the RV lifestyle, in case they change their mind. With property stored someplace, you can have peace and be assured that your valuable possessions are safe and being taken care of. This is much better than dragging them all over during your adventures.

So before setting out for your road trip, take time to decide on how you would handle the issue of possessions.

This will ensure that you do not make any decisions that you will regret later.

Choosing an RV That is Suitable for You

When you have limited living space, privacy and comfort are essential things to consider. You must ensure that you select a large enough unit to meet your needs and will also ensure your comfort. If not, you will find yourself miserable on a trip that you should enjoy.

RVs are considered for traveling and living in different kinds of places and in all sorts of weather. For this reason, you must choose an RV that is suitable for all kinds of weather. You must ensure that it will be good for you in all kinds of changes in temperature from hot to cold weather.

To make things easier for you, you can join an RV group where you can have access to all sorts of information with regards to RVs. This information can be accessed from magazines and books. With the information, you will be able to know the ratings of temperature for every RV as well as their model, the year they were made, and its make.

You may spend a bit of money getting in these RV groups, but it is better than making the wrong RV choice and regretting it later.

Where to Set Up Home Base

A lot of RVers usually set up a home base by buying and developing land that is properly zoned, acquiring an RV lot on a deed, or renting a campsite for a long period of time.

With a home base, you have the opportunity to have a permanent address and some sense of security as well. It is, however, not necessary to have a home base.

Some people just rent space in every region where they visit. When you have a home base, you might be required to pay some fee on a daily, weekly, or monthly basis. It may seem simple, but it can also be very costly for you. This is because when staying at a campsite for a short time, you will be required to pay more than you would have to if you were living there for a longer time.

Tony and I have traveled all over and have not set up a home base. We found this as a better option because we would often find cheap campsite locations and some for free.

Therefore, for you to make the right decision, you ought to do extensive research and find out which campsite would be financially suitable for you for the period that you would want to stay there. This way, you will be able to fully decide if having a home base is really necessary.

Living With Kids in an RV

So, you have kids, and you are wondering if it is a good idea to go on the trip with them. Well, that is a big consideration that you have to make.

Well, in my opinion, if you are planning on living in an RV on a full-time basis, taking kids with you may not be a good choice. This is because RV campsites may not be the best places you would want to have your kids staying in terms of safety. In fact, most of them barely have any resources suitable for kids.

Also, having a lot of people in one RV may bring about major problems and discomfort. Imagine your kids in need of running around like they do at home and still do not have the space to do so? This might be disastrous for you as a parent.

RVs also have limited space. When you choose to go with your kids, consider extra storage space for their toys, clothes, equipment, medication, as well as food. This will definitely take up space in your living area.

This is not to say that living in an RV with kids is not possible. It very much is, but you will find it very challenging. You can travel with them everywhere. However, be ready for some extra work and responsibility in your journey. It will be so complicated compared to traveling with just one other person.

RV Living with Pets

A lot of people like to take their pets with them on an RV tour. They enjoy keeping their pets around as they travel.

It is, however, important to know that pets, just like kids, can give you a handful of work to do. This is because they also need food, toys, equipment, and medication. Such things need a lot of space for storage, which would otherwise be used for other essential items.

It is also important to know that some parks have a no pet policy. For this reason, some campers have been asked to pay extra charges or camp in designated areas. For you to travel with your pet, you need to do a lot of research to find out which campgrounds are best for you and your fur baby.

Also, keep in mind how much havoc pets can cause in an RV. If you are not careful, you will have to deal with pet odor in your RV, ticks, fleas. and fur all over, as well as damaged cabinets and upholsters.

You may also risk termination of your stay at a campground if you do not pick up their waste or if they are a nuisance to other campers. Termination may mean ejection from the campground without any refund.

In our journey over the years, we have seen successful RV living with pets. Most of the pets that are lucky enough to be carried along on a trip are small dogs that can be washed and groomed regularly. Their owners also take them along when going to run their errands. In our experience, we have not come across someone successfully RVing with large pets. Some have even carried their pigs along. However, this may make the trip less fun for you in the long-run.

Mail-Forwarding Service

As always, it is very important to keep in touch with the outside world, even when taking an adventure in your RV. This is for the sake of maintaining a healthy relationship with your family, friends, and acquaintances in the business world. Fortunately, staying in touch with the outside world has become easier than before. These days, a laptop that is well connected, a smartphone, and a mail forwarding service will be enough to keep you adequately connected.

You can get mail forwarding services at the cost of about $10 every month, including postage. With this service, you can be assured of convenience and the safety of your mail. Also, with the mail forwarding service, you can earn legal citizenship in the state where the service is situated.

Rates of forwarding services vary for every state. For instance, Texas and Florida may have cheaper rates than California and New York.

Signing up is not a complicated task. All you need to do is select the forwarding service that you would like to use and handing in a formal request stating the change of address from your previous post office to the current.

When the mail forwarding service is available to you, your incoming letters will be sent from the post office to the mail forwarding service. The previous address will cease to be active; thus, mail won't be sent to it. Once the forwarding service has your mail, it will contact you for information on where you would like the letters sent.

The good thing about the mail forwarding service is that you can start and stop it whenever you like. However, it is important that you do your research about them since each company has its own governing rules and regulations.

Tony and I used The Good Sam Club, which was very helpful and convenient in delivering our mail whenever and wherever we went.

Like everything else, the mail forwarding system has its own flaws. With it, you will have to wait a little longer for your mail as there is usually some delay before delivery. Also, it may cost a bit more than the monthly payment because you have to pay postage fees.

Besides those flaws, a mail forwarding service is a good option for anyone wishing to have a home base and have no one at home to receive their mail. It is also very reliable and safe to use.

Insurance

Insurance is an important issue. Especially if you plan on RVing for a long time or on a full-time basis. Well, fortunately, having insurance as an RVer is similar to everybody else.

If you plan to have a home base, however, it is crucial that you carry your health insurance policy everywhere. This will help by providing you with coverage everywhere you go. It is also wise to note that some companies will not provide insurance coverage if you are not in the same state as your mail forwarding service. These companies include limited service-area policies as well as HMOs.

Some types of insurance you will need include health insurance, automobile insurance, RV insurance, and a roadside assistance policy. Most Americans who are working full-time jobs usually receive medical insurance benefits through their employer. You may be considered retired or self-employed, so this becomes a bit trickier for a full-time nomad to obtain.

First, establish a state of residence. You can establish this via your mail forwarding service or by having a brick and mortar house that you still live in at least part-time. Florida has the best options for establishing yourself as a resident of this state. There is no state income tax, and they have medical insurance plans that also work "out of network" better than most other plans. (See Florida Blue when you are doing your insurance research.)

Secondly, examine your options. As of 2020, you can still obtain insurance coverage from the Affordable Healthcare Act marketplace. You can contact a licensed agent for any major health insurance carrier such as Blue Cross/ Blue Shield and get a quote. There are a variety of discount programs for medical care and prescriptions that will also work in a pinch if you're a generally healthy person.

Thirdly, get automobile insurance. You already have to register your car in a home state of residence. Most states require proof of insurance in order to keep your vehicle registered anyway. Keep proof of that insurance on your person. You should also carry RV insurance, especially if that vehicle needs to have its own registration tag. Popular auto insurance carriers such as Progressive, Liberty Mutual, and State Farm also offer roadside assistance policies that can call you a tow truck when you're in a jam.

You could also consider joining AAA or AARP. AAA offers its members not just roadside assistance but also "trip ticks" or maps of suggested routes, travel discounts, and accommodation or attraction discounts all over the country. My husband and I have been members of AAA for years, and I would highly recommend it.

Part 2: RV Life for Novices

10 Common RV Mistakes

Everybody makes mistakes in life. The RV world is just like any other, with occasional mistakes that are usually made. Mistakes aren't made by newbies alone, but by experienced RV campers as well. Once in a while, they also forget to do crucial activities such as forget to carry in the RV cover or fasten the pantry well.

If you're following along in this book, then you'll have the kind of RV you want, and you'll be a pro at the terminology of the RV world. You should also have your insurance squared away, have a mail forwarding service established, and have organized your belongings to fit in the camper.

Sadly, there are mistakes about RV life that are dangerous and could cost someone a lot, including their lives. So, to be able to avoid these pitfalls that may bring about unpleasant experiences in your RV camping trip, here are a few mistakes you should avoid.

Campsite Etiquette

Many people are different and have different things they like. That is why it is good to be considerate of others' needs and respect their boundaries. I will discuss campsite etiquette in much more detail in a later chapter.

While at the campsite, it is a good practice to observe campsite etiquette as well as respect your neighbors. Lack of doing so may make you a bad campsite neighbor. For instance, you could be the sort of camper who makes noise for the neighbors at night, does not pick up his or her pet's waste, or carelessly empties their tanks, leaving a messy place at the campground.

All these habits will make you a bad campsite neighbor. Nobody likes living next to a bad neighbor. For this reason, it is best to observe the rules and be the best neighbor you can be in the small campground community around you. When you are considerate of others, you are likely to make new friends. Making new friends has been one of the highlights of our travels.

Not to mention that if you are a "bad" neighbor, you're probably breaking a few rules of conduct of the campground and might get evicted.

Not Bringing in the Awning

The awning is imperative when traveling with an RV as it protects one from harsh weather, provides shade, and ensures privacy in campsites that are cramped up. While it is great, this accessory is very fickle and so easy to forget on your RV.

When on your trip, you could come across high winds that could change a very good awning into a bundle of torn fabric and bent metal. For this reason, stash your awning once you detect any sign of bad weather. Everything changes, including the weather.

Don't forget the awning when you're packing up your campsite. Make sure you keep a checklist of pack up items for heading out. It's really easy to not give the awning a second thought as you're packing up to head out of a campsite.

Driving the RV Improperly

Most people assume that because they have a driver's license, they are good at driving RVs, too. Well, I have to be the one to burst your bubble, but RVs are not cars.

These vehicles are longer, taller, and weigh more than the cars you are used to. For this reason, it is essential that you consider learning how to drive one before you set out for your journey.

It's important that you learn how to properly drive your RV. When you learn, you will realize that RVs have their own techniques when it comes to things like turning, backing up, and slowing down when the winds are high.

Do not rush into driving your vehicle once you purchase the RV. Take some time and practice often before you start your trip. Most driving schools offer RV classes. In case you have a friend with an RV, you could also ask them to help you with tips and tricks on driving the RV well.

Do not assume that you can drive an RV simply because you can comfortably maneuver around with your car. Keep in mind that RVs are different!

Not Leveling the RV

I would not enjoy sleeping on an angle. Neither would I enjoy walking upward as if on a hill while inside the RV, or shower in a slanted bathroom. I bet you would not either.

For this reason, it is best to simply level the RV. Leveling an RV varies depending on the type of RV you have. However, some people overlook this process in the assumption that campgrounds are leveled. Well, this is not the case. Campgrounds, even the fancy ones, are not leveled well enough for an RV. For this reason, take the process and level your RV as required.

You should follow the manufacturer's recommendations on how to level your particular RV. There are also a number of leveling blocks and chocks on the market to assist you with leveling and stabilizing. Take the time to do this correctly, not only for your comfort but for the lifespan of your RV.

Not Disconnecting Cables

On one of our trips, my husband and I forgot to disconnect an electrical cord. We ended up driving 3 miles down the road dragging the cord behind us. It was not a good experience as others we passed were waving or honking at us, but we had no idea what the problem was.

Maybe you have seen an RV dragging a sewage hose or a cord just like we did. If you have not, do not be surprised. This is a common mistake that RVers make. Sometimes leaving a campground entails a lot from checking out to packing up your stuff. There is always a lot to remember. However, one of the things you should check before leaving is that all cords are disconnected and that you are not dragging any behind. Do not be like us. Disconnect your cords!

Over Packing

It is obvious that when traveling, you can be tempted to pack a lot of stuff. We women tend to think too far ahead and carry things for future possibilities.

Also, if there is enough room in the RV, why not carry everything? Well, this may sound like a good idea, but it is important to note that there is a weight limit to what you can carry in an RV. If you exceed this limit, your trip will not be as fun as anticipated. This is because you will have a hard time driving and stopping your vehicle. The weight can also be risky for you and other people driving around your RV.

It is good to pack luggage of a reasonable amount and not throw in all sorts of baggage, which you may not even need. To make packing easier, write down a list of the necessary things you want to pack before packing, check your list several times, and cancel out on the things that you do not find necessary for the trip. This will make it easier for you to carry only the necessary things.

Not Defrosting the Freezer

I know this may sound like a minor issue, but this can be quite a big deal in the life of your fridge/freezer.

When it comes to freezers, RV freezers are not similar to household freezers. In RV freezers, ice builds up over time and consumes the storage space that was there initially. This causes the freezer not to function efficiently.

For this reason, it is very important that you defrost the freezer. The defrosting process is very simple. You just switch the fridge off, remove the food in it, and allow the frost to melt. For faster defrosting, a hair drier or directing a fan onto the ice can be very helpful.

Forgetting to Doublecheck Everything

It is imperative that you check your RV several times before driving to any location. Before you get into the cockpit and drive, ensure that you have checked the RV properly.

Check the connection on the tow vehicle, the lights, the compartment doors outside, as well as the rig. Ensure that your satellite dish is in place, and all vents and windows are closed. Check inside the RV as well from cupboards, doors, the items stored, and everything else in the RV.

For assistance, you can use a checklist that will help you ensure everything is okay before setting off the road. Doing so could save you a lot of future problems that would otherwise occur.

Ignoring Small Problems

No matter how small the problem is, pay close attention to it and ensure that the problem is solved. This happens a lot, especially when you hit your rig on a wall or a pole, which could cause a dent and leaving a tiny hole on your rig, which creates a pathway for moisture to get into your rig, which could de-laminate your rig. Causing more problems than expected.

So, if you have something peeling off the edge of your rig, or an issue with your roof, or a leak somewhere, just stop and take care of that problem before it creates a bigger problem such as delamination, mold, and mildew, which can be avoided by just dealing with the situation.

Not Performing Proper Maintenance

Tires, pressure, and lug torque should be checked prior to every trip. Just because the tire has plenty of tread doesn't mean the tires are safe. Those tires might be 10 years old and full of dry rot. If you have a tire blow out while on the highway, it's not only frustrating but it can cause major damage to your RV.

RV Checklist

After traveling and living in an RV for years, I know it can be stressful to pack things for a trip. Knowing what to pack can be tricky for a person who is new in this world of adventure. However, with time, it gets easier to pack and carry things around while traveling.

As you already know by now, packing all that you want in some limited space can be very challenging. Also, if you carry too much, you may struggle with all the rattling items and the imbalance that the weight may cause. This can be annoying and very dangerous for everybody.

For this reason, it is important to only carry the necessary things that you need. Remember that you will also acquire more things along the way; therefore, you must always leave room for extra stuff that you are likely to pick up.

To assist you in packing and ease you of all the stress, below is a checklist of the very necessary items that you need to carry with you on your trip. This checklist includes essentials, kitchen equipment, groceries, RV accessories, as well as clothing and personal items.

RV Essentials

These are the things that you must carry. These are very necessary for making your life comfortable during the trip.

- Surge protector
- Shovel
- Flashlight
- Electrical adapters
- Leveling blocks
- Electrical and duct tape
- Water pressure regulator
- Wheel chocks
- Battery jumper cables
- RV-friendly toilet paper
- Toilet chemicals

- Extra cotter pins

- Sewer kit

- Extra motor oil and transmission fluid

- Large bag with zipping for documents like registration, license, and reservations, etc.

- Tire pressure gauge

- Drinking water hose

- Fire extinguisher

- Extension cords

- Emergency road kit

Emergency Items

Safety is a very important thing to consider. No matter where you are going, you could have an emergency that may need some medical attention. In addition, you will have some peace of mind if you know that you have your emergency kit already.

To ensure that you carry everything that you need, write a list of needs that are helpful in case of an emergency. The items in your list could include:

- A fire extinguisher

- Medications

- Smoke detectors

- Carbon monoxide detector

- Fully stocked first aid kit

- Emergency Hand-Crank / Solar Radio

- LED Flashlight

- Hand Warmers

- Waterproof Matches

- Emergency Candles

- Waterproof Poncho

- Green Lightstick – 12 Hour

Food

So, in your first days, you may not be well conversant with the sort of foods you should carry. You may not know the amount that you must carry. Well, the kind of food and the amount to carry along totally depends on the length of the trip, the place where you are going, and the storage space available.

For instance, you can find RVs with refrigerators as big as the fridges in residential homes. These fridges can hold a large amount of food. When traveling, remember to carry a lot of water, snacks, and food items that you will use when going on your adventures. As for water, do not depend fully on your tank or city water. Rather, carry extra bottles and gallons of water.

Amongst the foods you can carry are:

- Eggs

- Vegetables and fruits

- Drink mix packets

- Grill meats like burgers and hot dogs

- Bread
- Canned foods
- Butter mixes
- Condiments, including mayo, mustard, ketchup, etc.
- Frozen, dried meals
- Salt
- Butter or margarine
- Peanut butter and jelly
- Cereal
- Baking items
- Pepper, spices, and herbs
- Snacks
- Cooking oil/ spray

- Soups

It is important to note that some of these ingredients, such as eggs, are things that you can also acquire at any grocery shop in every part of the country. For this reason, you do not need to pack a lot of them.

My advice would be to consider where you are going for how long and create a menu or a general meal plan. That will help you determine what food to bring on your trip.

Household and Kitchen Items

Kitchen items are good because you do not have to keep purchasing them every other time during your journey. Knives, pans, and pots last very long. In case you do not have a pressure cooker, it is best to consider getting one. These pots are usually very familiar with RVers because it saves them from buying some other equipment.

If you are a lover of coffee, it would be best not to forget your coffee maker. There is nothing as awesome as sitting outdoors, listening to the sound of the forest, and feeling the breeze while sipping a hot cup of coffee.

So, some of the kitchen items that you could carry include:

- Bowls, plates, and cups
- Water bottles
- Dishtowels
- Garbage bags
- Can opener
- Zip close bags
- Chopping board
- Soapdish
- Potholders
- Skillets
- Plastic wrap
- Utensils/cutting knives
- Disinfecting wipes
- Paper towels

- Napkins

- Cooler

- Tongs and skewers

- Food storage container

- Camping griddle and pie iron

- Matches and lighter

Clothing and Bedroom Stuff

This is the trickiest part for most people. This is because a lot of people usually think about the weather and its changes before they set out for the journey.

To handle this menace easily, you can carry clothes that are light and are suitable for any occasion. Some of these clothes are pants that are waterproof, which you can put on a windbreaker or another pair of pants. You can also use them to block the wind and keep you warm. You can also carry one or two thick pairs of socks, along with some firm shoes. Depending on the season, you can also carry a hat to keep you from the sun's rays.

Other things you could carry are:

- Shoes, including sneakers, hiking boots, sandals, etc.
- Underwear
- Sheets and blankets
- Pillows
- Clothes hangers
- Bathing suit
- Sewing kit
- Short and long sleeve t-shirt
- Rain gear
- Pants and shorts
- Sweatshirts and jackets
- Towels

- Socks

- Alarm clock

Toys and Gadgets

Toys are fun and healthy at the same time. They bond people together through fun activities. If you are going on a trip with your kids, it would be good to pack these gadgets to keep them from getting bored. You can also pack a few things to keep you occupied when out camping. However, be keen to ensure that you do not overpack.

Some of these things include:

- Frisbee

- Books and magazines

- Hula-hoops, corn hole, horseshoes, etc. for yard games.

- Playing cards

- Wood

- Notepad or journal

- Fishing gear, plus license, tackle, rods, etc.

- Guitar

- Puzzles

- Camping chairs

- Hatchet or saw

- Radio

- Binoculars

- Flotation devices

- Sports equipment, including baseball, basketball, football, etc.

- Headphones

- Laptop

Toiletries and Personal items

These are things that are essential when traveling for a long journey. Most of these are things that you cannot do without. They ensure the comfort of your trip.

These toiletries and personal items are:

- Toothbrush

- Toothpaste

- Batteries

- Medications and prescriptions

- Phone chargers

- Shampoo and conditioner

- Cash and credit cards

- Travel map and campground directory

- First-aid kit

- Contact lenses or glasses

- Reservation confirmations
- Watch
- Lotion
- Sunscreen
- Shaving gel
- Comb and brush
- Bug spray
- Makeup
- Nail clippers
- Floss
- Deodorant
- Razor
- Watch
- Sunglasses

- Hair ties

- Soap

What to Leave Behind

There are some things that you can do without on the long RV trip like heavy books. Instead of cramping them up in your RV, you can use the contemporary method of reading ebooks that are readily available online.

In the first year of our trip, my husband Tony, who loves reading, carried so many books, some of which he never got to even read. So, we met a few friends who encouraged us to do away with the old school way of doing things and embrace the new trends. With time, we got used to ebooks and audiobooks found online. Now we have fewer books and more space in our RV.

Other things that you can do without include work out equipment. You may be a lover of fitness and want to continue with your daily work out routines. Well, that may be good, but you will be surprised that once you are on the road, you may never use the equipment. Also, there are so many activities that you will do during camping that will still keep you fit. For example, hiking and swimming can be activities that will help you get enough exercise during the long trip.

Ladies, this may hurt a little, but high-heeled shoes should be left behind. Let's face it; you may never get to use them during your trip. Most of the places that you will go to are not good for high heels; hence they may cause you to break or twist your ankle. For you and your ankles' sake, leave the heels behind.

Documents to Carry

There are documents that you should always have in your RV while traveling around. These documents are essential as they have important information that may be needed in case of an emergency. Now, carrying them does not mean that you are pessimistic and anticipating a problem: however, it is good to always be prepared.

These documents include:

Medical Papers

It is of utmost importance to carry several medical documents with you during your trip. These would be very helpful during an emergency and would help police officers, firefighters, or paramedics help you better and faster. Unfortunately, something fatal may occur, causing you to pass out and not have the ability to speak and express yourself. For this reason, it is important that you have your medical records with you to make work easier for those who may want to help you. With the information, they can also manage to help you without giving you medication that could make things worse for you. Please do not assume that things will always be fine. It is good that you be ready.

These documents include hospitalization and surgical histories, health insurance, names and contacts of your current doctor, allergies, prescribed medication that you currently have, as well as any legal records entailing your medical care, such as a power of attorney.

Documents on Insurance

You should always carry insurance information that covers your health and vehicles.

Vehicle-related Documents

These documents include license and information on registration, titles, travel insurance cards, vehicle insurance cards, and information regarding roadside assistance.

For this reason, if you face a problem with regards to your vehicle or, unfortunately, have an accident, this information will be very important to help you get the assistance that you need.

Addresses

When you are away from home, having a copy of people's names and addresses can be very convenient.

While away, you may need to contact one of your neighbors or friends back at home to help you with something important. This could be anything from sorting out some bills or checking your mail; you will need someone to help you with these tasks. For this reason, it is good to have their contacts.

It is good that you have your contacts stored in your smartphone; however, it is very important to also have your friends' email addresses since you may lose signal while out on an adventure.

With the hard copies of contacts and email addresses, you can be sure that you will be able to constantly keep in touch with them and get the information and help that you may need.

Pet Information

If you wish to travel with your pet(s), you also need to carry information about it. This is because your pet is very much like you when it comes to some issues to do with health. For this reason, you ought to carry documents like your pet's medical records, list of foods, list of medications, list of allergies, information regarding inoculation, and the family veterinarian's contact information.

While on the road, it is vital that your pet's collar has its identification tags. This will help people contact you easily and help you get your pet back in case it gets lost.

Legal Papers

When going on your trip, you should never forget to carry copies of your legal papers. If you are traveling for an extended time or going full nomad, you should carry copies of your vehicle title, marriage license, military separation papers, divorce papers, health care, and living will documents, passports, deeds, birth certificates, powers of attorney, emergency contacts, as well as the contact information of your attorney.

With this information, you can ensure extra protection in case anything happens to you. You can be surprised how much this information can help when out on the road.

One time, Tony and I had an emergency that needed the attention of our attorney. Luckily, my husband had carried his contact information in his diary, and it saved us a load of work. It would have taken us days to solve the matter, but because we had the information, we got it solved in a few hours.

Therefore, do not ignore the importance of this information. It can save your life!

Information on Tech

To handle your banking and online issues easily while on the road, you will need to take with you some papers that hold information regarding the operating system, model, and brand of your computer, passwords, cell phone, virus protection program, and the GPS system. Don't forget to keep a hard copy of the pass

Without this information, it may be challenging to access online services or deal with your technical issues.

Information and Guides About Your RV

Every RV comes with a guide, which provides vast information on handling the RV. This is more like a coaching tool by the manufacturer that will help you deal with arising issues in the RV like mechanical problems. For this reason, it is important that you carry these documents with you while traveling around in your RV.

There are also camping guides that are very helpful when traveling around. For instance, The Good Sam Travel and Savings Guide and RVer's Friend have been very helpful to us in the past years as it has provided us with a lot of information regarding RV camping. From it, we found campsite locations, RV service shops, as well as information on getting important documents such as fishing licenses. These guides have a lot of information that would be helpful as well as make your RV life more comfortable and fun.

Campsite Etiquette Tips

Everyone likes having a good neighbor around them. Whether at home or in a campsite somewhere in the woods, everyone values a neighbor that respects their privacy and gets along with them. Being the good neighbor that everyone desires is not a hard task. The campsites are especially easy places to be a good neighbor because most people are like-minded and look forward to bonding and offering their help.

It is important to keep in mind that you are not the only one at the campsite using the resources provided. There are also other like-minded people who are there to have a good time. Therefore, respect the people and the campsite, leaving it as clean and orderly as you found it. Ensure that you are courteous and follow the rules at the campsite.

For instance, when disposing of your tanks, it is campsite etiquette to dispose of it at the right spot and leave your spot as clean as you found it without any odors, food, or waste.

Also, respecting other people's need for silence at night is courteous and good as campsite etiquette. Otherwise, you would be considered as a bad neighbor and risk the cancellation of your stay at the campsite, possibly with no refund.

I bet you would want the same of your campsite neighbors. It is everybody's desire that they are treated with kindness and respect. Since you are traveling and looking forward to making memories and meeting new people, you would also love for your alone time to be peaceful. To ensure that you are treated with kindness, it is important to respect everybody's space at the camp. Remember, do unto others as you would like them to do to you.

Observe the Rules

This is the most basic campsite etiquette that you can ever find. When you get into any campsite, there is always a copy of the rules and regulations that you will be given.

When you adhere to these basic rules, you will have hacked one of the requirements of living in a campsite in peace. You will also make things easier for the people operating the campsite as well as the neighbors around you.

Most of these rules are for your own good and for the good of other neighbors around you. For instance, to ensure safety, there is a rule regulating the speed limits on the roads of the campsite. There are also specific times when the campsite should be quiet. At such times, things like generators and outdoor lights should be switched off. This is because most people want their peace at that time and want to relax from a long day of adventure.

Keep the Neighborhood Tidy

Yes, this is very important. While living in an RV, you will realize that a lot of RVers are usually easy going in character. However, it is awkward to find things lying around the compound. Anything considered trash should be well disposed to continue keeping the place clean.

Sewer Connections

Connect to them as required but make the connections as secure as possible. Most connections to sewers usually face your neighbor's area. For this reason, it is good to use hoses that are in good condition and not torn. Also, observing care and discretion is good etiquette at the campsite area.

Mind Your Pet

When your pet poops around the compound, it is your duty to pick after them. Literally!

You are also responsible for stopping dogs from barking excessively and disturbing the peace of the other campers at the campsite. It is important to note that not everyone loves dogs. For this reason, unnecessary barking by your dog could annoy your neighbors and bring about conflict, making your stay at the campsite uncomfortable and less fun.

When you take proper care of your pet and control its actions, you will be considered a good neighbor and appreciated at the campsite. Remember to use a leash on your dog so you may have an easier time keeping tabs on them and keep them from causing a mess at the campsite.

Late Arrival

There are times that you may get to the campsite late at night. When you do so, it is best to maintain peace at the campsite. It is definitely not always easy to set up things stealthily; however, it is worth trying.

When setting up your RV and settling down at the campsite, ensure that you respect others' wishes to have peace and keep the noise at a minimum. It is understandable that you need to park and settle down at the campsite. Most of your neighbors have probably been in the same situation. However, most will not appreciate noisy set-ups full of banging doors, noisy conversations, or contentions on how the RV should be leveled. When in such a situation, do the essential things first and leave the rest for the following day.

This should also be applied when leaving the campsite early in the morning. Ensure that your departure does not cause a nuisance to other campers around you. This way, you will leave the campsite courteously without being a nuisance to your fellow RVers.

Campfires

Every campsite has rules that govern the placement, control, and use of campfires. Before lighting one, find out what the rules dictate about them. Ensure that you know if they are even permitted on the premises.

Also, avoid using your firepit as your trash can. You do not want to leave the firepit trashy with food remains from dinner or cans of beer. It is best to use the fire pit for campfires only and leave them as you found them for the next camper to also enjoy using them.

I bet you would also want to find a clean firepit. For this reason, ensure that you keep it just like you would like to find it.

Parking the Rig

Parking the rig at the campsite is sometimes a very clear task to do. You may even find a cement pad at the campsite. However, in many circumstances, the only posts guiding you will be the sewer and electric hookup. To observe etiquette, you need to pack your rig on your side of the hookup. Do not slide out and take up the space of your neighbor's spot.

To make this easier, check out the campsite map and find the right bearing for your rig. Alternatively, you could check out other campers' rigs and find out how they have packed their rigs. Check to see if their rigs are close to the hookups or at the center of their spots. When you pack in the same way as your neighbors, you will manage to get better spacing, just like your neighbors.

We have gone to campgrounds, where RVers did not pack the same due to the difference in site dimensions and shape. In such situations, every camper had to try their best and fit the rig properly into their site. While people park differently, sometimes, it is good to ensure that you observe fairness in the way you park and not take up someone else's space.

Ensure that you leave space enough to guarantee you and your neighbors the room and privacy that they deserve. In this case, you will have to use common sense as it is crucial in observing campground etiquette.

No Trespassing

In our first year at an RV campsite, we had a neighbor who had lost his map to the campground. I believe it had been blown away by the wind, and he was trying to find it. We were really surprised when he approached us while we were basking in the sun and requested if he could look around our place. It was a surprise because we had not considered the site we were on to be our place. However, he was respectful enough to ask for our permission. You can bet that a great friendship ensued from there between us and our neighbor's family. We really appreciated his respect.

Among the unwritten campsite code of conduct is to respect other peoples' sites and consider them as their homes just like you would when living at home. I believe you would find it awkward to walk around your neighbor's home compound at any time of the day without asking for permission. If anything, you would look very suspicious.

Therefore, it is important to respect other campers' space and not trespass on the sites that are occupied. When a camper is on a certain site, the site belongs to him or her as long as they stay at the campsite.

For this reason, stay on the marked pathways when taking a stroll around the park. Ensure that you do not invade or disturb other RVers by trespassing on "their" property.

Cleaning Your RV

Due to high water bills, and the mess water can bring about in a site, most campgrounds do not permit cleaning

RVs at the site. For this reason, it is important that you understand the rules.

To ensure your RV's cleanliness, you can use a waterless cleaner or a small bucket of water and a rag. This will only ensure minimal cleanliness of your RV. You will only clean out the spots and dust it off a little.

If you are lucky enough to be in a campground that permits washing RVs, ensure that you properly use the opportunity given. Do not leave the water flowing and waste the water that could otherwise be used by other campers. Spray the water on your rig and do not splash over your neighbor's rig. You may be surprised that they do not have an interest in cleaning their RV as you clean yours.

Also, it is good to inform your neighbor when you are about to clean your rig so they can do the necessary things to keep their property from getting wet. This will be courteous and will ensure good etiquette at the campground. It may also improve your relationship with your neighbor. You may even make a new friend!

The Golden Rule

"Do unto others as you would have them do unto you."

This is the rule of thumb. If the campground rules and etiquette are not so clear to you, you could do this instead. Consider what you would like other campers to do to you.

How would you like to be treated? What would you consider to be etiquette at the campground? Whatever answers you have to those questions, implement them. If you think there is something that may disturb your neighbor's peace, just walk over to them and ask them about it.

Also, if your neighbors do not observe etiquette and are constantly disturbing your peace, the best thing to do is to handle the situation with the utmost politeness. If you do not succeed in handling the issue, you can always find another campground with better rules and better neighbors. Remember, you are not stuck in a house. You are in a mobile home - just move!

RV Life Logistics

Living in an RV is different from living at home. There are things that you will have to consider when you make up your mind to live in your RV. There are things that will have to do to live your RV life just like you would when at home. There are logistics that you will need to know and plan ahead for so that your life may be comfortable in your RV.

Small Spaces

When you move into your RV, there are things in life that will most definitely change. There are comforts that you will have to forego because the RV is not like your home. For instance, having a warm bath in a bathtub. Believe me. You will miss some of those comforts.

I miss taking care of my garden and having my friends over for a big party in my backyard. I miss constant hot showers and the fast internet connection I had at home. However, these are comforts and luxuries that I have come to learn to let go of. I have learned not to care about them as much. My priorities have changed.

All these things are awesome, and you will miss them but they are nothing compared to the fun you will have when embarking on adventures all over the country. While the space is small in an RV, it will never deprive you of your comforts. With time, you will get used to the limited space and adjust.

You will also have the benefit of easily maintaining cleanliness in your space. You will not have so much to take care of every day. If you used to struggle with keeping your home clean, believe me, an RV will make you feel more organized than ever because you will manage to keep the place clean.

Staying Connected

Internet is not such a tricky service to get when traveling in an RV. You can tether from your phone like my husband, and I do from time to time or have a data plan from your cell phone provider. Internet services can be found in many states. For instance, we used Verizon and I can attest to the fact that it has served us well. You can find it in most states.

When traveling, you will discover that there is wifi in most RV campgrounds. However, due to connection issues and use by a lot of people, you may struggle with it since it can be really slow. For better and faster internet service, I highly recommend buying a cell booster, which will amplify your cell signal. Even though you may go to places with low signal, you will have amplified signal with a cell booster. You can use boosters like a WeBoost cell booster. This will make a tremendous difference in enabling you to gain access to the internet in isolated areas.

For TV entertainment, you can borrow DVDs from other campers around you or use Netflix, which has a wide variety of entertaining programs. You will also find cable or antenna hookups on most RVs as well as the parks. These will enable you to get entertainment from TVs easily.

Dumping waste

In RVs, you will find tanks where most waste is stored. These are the black, grey, and the freshwater tanks. There are, however, composite toilets in the campgrounds that most RVers use.

Toilet waste is stored in the black tank, whereas the water from the shower or sinks is stored in the grey tank.

About 60 gallons of fresh water is stored in the freshwater tank. In the black and grey tanks, there are little hose pipes that connect with the sewer. When dumping your tank, you need to pull the levers as indicated in both tanks to the sewer. It is not as complicated as it may appear, but some people don't always get it right.

Finding Places to Camp

While traveling in an RV, you will be required to stay in an RV campground often. It depends on where you are and what you are up to. My husband and I have spent a lot of time on the west coast in so many RV parks in the region. Your other option is to boondock, which may not be as convenient a choice. As I shared earlier, you will find a lot of amenities in RV parks from wifi internet (although it is slow), swimming pools in some parks, bathrooms, as well as showers.

You can get different types of RV and trailer parks in different regions. For instance, retirees stay in posh RV resorts, whereas the young and young at heart stay at more rustic campgrounds.

Every park charges a different amount of fee per night. We have found parks charging $30 for every night while others charge more. The charges vary in each park with the more comfortable ones having much higher charges.

Keeping Fit

Most people like to exercise to ensure that they keep fit in their daily lives. Well, you can also keep fit while traveling around in an RV. You can go for a run, take a walk, or even do push-ups in your RV. You can also find all sorts of workouts online that can guide you in your occasional exercises.

There are also gyms that are located all over the country, such as Planet Fitness. You can acquire membership from any of them and gain access to the gym in the states that you are going to visit. In these gyms, you can have access to the facilities and workouts. Some gyms also have tootsie rolls and massage chairs that are freely accessible to members.

Not to mention that a gym membership also comes with access to the changing rooms and shower facilities. Even if you choose not to take up some weights, you can take a nice hot shower.

Doing Laundry

When we first hit the road, I had only packed about ten shirts for my husband. There was not much room in the RV, so we did not pack up a lot of clothes. We tried our best to pack light as we had read in a certain RV guide. The guide was a great inspiration and gave us a lot of help.

When it came to doing laundry, we found an RV campground with a laundry room. After a while, we were able to purchase a portable washing machine and dryer that have really helped us throughout our journey. However, the portable washer and dryer can be a little stressful as they are small, so you cannot wash or dry a lot of clothes in them at one time.

Voting

When traveling in an RV, there are some issues that RVers will think about. Voting is one of those issues. Many people ask me about voting while traveling. I have been asked questions like which station do you vote at when you are not at home? How do you gain access to a ballot box and cast your vote?

In 2004, a hot key topic arose about the permanent house issue. This arose when some RVers were cut from the polls since they had registered their address in Tennessee and Cleveland. Fortunately, this controversial issue has been solved, and you can be allowed to use whatever address you register as your "legal house" to cast your vote.

In this case, most RVers use the address on their mail forwarding service or their driver's license. Keep in mind that you have a right to vote and are allowed to cast your vote even though you do not have a permanent home made of bricks. Remember the jurisdiction that you are under as well as your housing status. Knowing these details will make the steps you have to take easier.

After knowing the location of your legal house, you will be required to get to an absentee ballot, which is more or less like it sounds. With the absentee ballot, you will be able to cast your vote even when absent from your jurisdiction. The absentee ballot is also your right. So, exercise it with all confidence.

To obtain an absentee ballot, there are different methods that you can use. You can contact the governmental offices or your local jurisdiction, and they will be able to direct you on what you need to get the absentee ballot. There are also other alternative outlets that can offer you assistance, in case your jurisdiction is slow in giving you direction. Such outlets are like VOTE.org, which can get the vote out for people who are not able to vote for some reason. This website offers a lot of assistance by registering voters, offering guidance to absentee voters in various states, giving information on absentee voting rules and regulations, offering assistance in checking your voter status, as well as examining different laws about your voter ID. This website will be very helpful in case you have a problem with acquiring your absentee ballot.

When you want to get an absentee ballot, it is best that you give the process plenty of time. Take time to request a ballot, get it, and mail it back. If you can, request the absentee ballot as soon as they are available. Do not contact your local jurisdiction a few days before the election and assume that you will acquire a ballot overnight. Plan for this if you plan to be away from your home jurisdiction for a while and will not be around during the election season.

Colorado and other states usually mail out ballots to their residents automatically throughout the year when votes are about to happen. Your voting on the road will be made easier if your home state is one of those states. Find out from your jurisdiction.

Remember that it is your constitutional right to vote, despite being on the road constantly. Ensure that you know your voting status and request for the absentee ballot early enough. Also, make sure that the ballot gets into the mail as soon as possible.

You protect the integrity of your democratic society for all future Americans when you play your part. Whether you are living in your RV on a full time or part-time basis and will not manage to cast your vote in person. Ensure that you exercise your right.

Money Matters

My husband and I initially had no idea that someone could make money while traveling. With time, however, other RV owners gave us ideas on how to make money while on the road. They gave us ideas that sounded a lot more fun than working in an office. There are various jobs available in every states, and you could take up several of them as you travel. Some of our friends found jobs from online job boards, where they found several jobs that can be done while traveling.

After we realized how much we cherished this RV life, we have constantly done online jobs and satisfied our clients through our services. Since a lot of people really love adventure but do not have the ability to travel as we have, we have taken several videos showing the beauty of nature for clients that wanted to show it on their online platforms like blogs. My husband also gives guidance online to clients who would like to travel all over but have no idea where to start. He also has RV guides online with helpful information on different topics.

Online jobs are not the only jobs available. You can also get jobs in various campgrounds or business places around the campground you are located in. There will always be a way for you to earn money while traveling. You just need to look for opportunities and offer exceptional services to your clientele.

Making Friends

Every RVer knows how easy it is to make friends in the RV world. This is due to how friendly RV campers are. Actually, it is rather typical for people with an interest in the same hobbies to connect with one other in a way. If you love art and pay a visit to an art gallery, you will most likely meet and link up with another lover of art. There is some sort of unspoken attraction that brings people with the same passion together. The case is not any different in the RV world. When traveling in an RV, you are most likely to meet another RVer who will be your friend.

Therefore, do not be astonished when you are welcomed by other RVers once you pull up to an RV campground. Some will offer you their assistance in backing your rig in and invite you for a campfire while enquiring where you are from. You can be certain that you will find help from someone in the park in case of any problems with your RV.

Whether you are a newbie or a seasoned veteran, you will find that the RV world is made up of fantastic people. My husband and I have made really great friends that have helped us a lot over the years that we have spent out RVing. Some have even taken an adventure and had a lot of fun with us in various states.

So, if you are wondering if you will make new friends along the journey, do not fret. The RV world has plenty of adventurous friends to link up with. Making a friend in this world is as easy as ABC. Here is how to do it.

Be the First to Make a Move

Yes, try it. It will not hurt. Be friendly, outgoing, and welcoming wherever you are located. Maybe it is not in your nature to be the one to make a move on a stranger first, but just give it a try. People are usually more willing to converse and interact when traveling. You may be surprised at how easy it is since a lot of campers at RV campgrounds are moving about trying to find people to link up with.

When we went to our first RV campground, we were invited over for a campfire by a couple that had been there for a few days. During our stay there, we formed a habit of sitting around the campfire every night and chatting about various topics. We shared experiences of our lives on the road as well as hacks to various things about RV life. While at the campfires, we met other campers that have been our close friends since then. Once in a while, we usually meet and have fun as well as help each other when problems arise. So, invite your neighbors to your campfire and make them your friends. You never know how close or helpful they will be in the future.

Join an RV Club

In the RV community, you will find a number of RV clubs where you can meet a lot of people and make friends. Such clubs include Fifth-Wheelers, Airstreamers, Solo RVers, Weekend Warriors, Van dwellers, RV brand clubs, Younger working RVers, among many more.

A lot of these clubs usually hold gatherings every year, which you can go to and make friends with. Sometimes you will be required to pay for entry to the gatherings, while at other times, you will gain entry for free.

Pick a club or two that you would want to be a part of and follow up on the gatherings that you would want to go to. For you to make friends, you will have to be active and make yourself a bit conspicuous. Everybody has a shy side and wants people to accept them. However, there are times that you need to burst out of that cocoon and make an effort to make new friends.

All groups are different and have different people. For this reason, take your time and pick one that suits your needs and with people who have the same interest as you.

Attend Campground Events

Joining an RV club and attending their events are two different things. You may be in an RV group but fail to attend their events. RV events are very helpful since you can regularly link up with other RV travelers at the events. Normally, campgrounds that are bigger and well established have a schedule of annual events that their customers may attend.

Some of these events include barbeques, game nights, and pool parties, among others. They are the perfect platforms to get more acquainted with your neighbors at the campground. Find out more about such events from the front office.

RVing full time has never been lonely for us. We always meet up with other people and have a lot of fun. We have come to be part of a community that is closer than any other community we have been part of. Therefore, if you plan to go on an RV trip, I am sure that you will make lots of friends.

Social Media

There is a reason why social media goes by its name. It was created for more than just scrolling down other peoples' feeds. It was meant for connecting people together and engaging them in different ways. It is the best platform for making friends or staying in touch with friends you have made.

When RVing, we met a lot of friends on Facebook. Thanks to our kids, we have learned a bit about Instagram and are still trying to maneuver through the platform. While we are not as active on Instagram as we are on Facebook, we have made a few friends that have been great. We follow a number of other RVers, and whenever we see any of them in the same location as us, we write them a direct message and get in touch. Since we also share our locations often, a lot of people usually message us as well.

Also, whenever we meet someone at campgrounds, breweries, or restaurants, we usually take note of their social media handles so that we can keep in touch. This helps us keep the bond tight even when we are a great distance apart.

When RVers link up, on whatever platform, there is usually an instant bond that occurs. We can comfortably share stories regarding different places we have been to, as well as the struggles we have faced. This is what makes the RV community so amazing. There is usually so much to talk about since RVing is so unique. As time passes by, it is becoming more prevalent and easy, thus have more RVers joining the platform. Most RVers also have a desire to link up with people with similar passions and experiences.

Because of friends that we have met on Facebook, we have formed relationships with great people who have become an integral part of our lives. Some of these friends have introduced us to other people, campgrounds, as well as RV clubs. Through them, we have had a lot of fun times and have acquired so much knowledge about RVing. Networking is easier in the RV world than in any other, if you ask me. With the help of social media, we have met a lot of people that we would otherwise have never met before.

So, do not worry. As long as you are in the RV world, making friends will be easy for you. Just take a step and ensure that you are available for other people to meet you.

RV Glamping

If you frequently go camping, you have probably heard of "glamping." This has risen to be one of the buzziest buzzwords ever in the outdoor world. It has emerged as a way of advancing the traditional ways of camping from the austere way of spending the night in secluded areas in the wilderness or in RVs at some parking lot. It has made camping posh and extravagant. However, it can be simplified to fit someone's budget and needs.

You have probably guessed by now that "glamping" is a mash-up of two words, i.e., "glamour" and "camping." It is simply adding a touch of glamour to your camping and making the experience more beautiful and luxurious. It is more like being in luxurious five-star hotel suites while out camping or just making your RV camping a bit more cozy than usual. This is a good way for a newbie RVer to be introduced to the RV world. You can also celebrate a special occasion by glamping in your RV.

The difference between the usual camping and glamping is the level of comfort. You may have campgrounds that have glamped up areas, which you can use at an obviously higher cost. When you make reservations at such campgrounds, you may acquire special amenities like showers that are spa-like or an extra closet in your tent where you can hang your clothes after you unpack. Every glamping experience is different depending on the campsite that you visit.

You can also glamp up your own space using some DIY glamping tips offered on many platforms online. You could do this by simply adding a more luxurious mattress, gastronomic cookware, or even a bigger tent.

Glamping your space can add some fun to your camping as you take part in decorating the space. There are so many simple things that can add a touch of glamour to your camping site from LED lights, an artsy rug, to an artistic camp chair.

Here is a list of a few glamping ideas that have worked for me, and I have seen other RVers use.

Custom Paint

RVs are not always very appealing to look at. Sometimes they can be too plain and ugly. So, one way you can glamp your RV is to do some custom paint that will make it more beautiful and appealing. You could also make your RV custom made to match your van or car.

Toy Hauler Deck

I have seen more people embracing toy hauler decks. I believe that they are going to totally revamp the RV industry as well as people's way of camping. Some companies have started embracing the idea and putting them in their RVs.

I have seen them on Class A RVs, some Class C RVs, Travel Trailers, and 5th wheels. It is true glamping when grilling some steaks or just relaxing in a spectacular spot while on your deck.

Lighting up Your Space

Among the things that influence one's mood is light. Lighting can set the mood to either good or bad. Lamps have, for a long time, been the most traditional kind of glamping lights. They add a nice soothing glow to a space when set on side tables as well as make the place look pretty.

Sometimes you may go to a location where electricity is not available. In case you find yourself in this situation, do not fret, LED lights can always work for you. You only need to place them wherever the bulbs would be. We have used rope lights at one time, which were somehow economical. You could stick them on to surfaces with a double-sided sticky tape and ensure that they are well secured. There are places with LED lights on the RV covers, thus making camping more beautiful. You could also use the traditional method of lanterns that are operated by battery.

Using Glamping Decor

You can use some fun detail to your RV space to add more dimension to it. To do this, you will need some additional pieces like figurines, vases, flowers, and picture frames. You can find some of these things at the dollar store, which has amazing lightweight portrait frames that you can use to hang different products. There are also vases at the store that you can use to put some decorative wildflowers to decorate your space.

Add Cozy Beddings to Your Bed

Spoiler alert - mattresses in RVs are not comfortable. We currently bought a memory foam mattress and a foam pad to put over the provided mattress. To add some glam to your RV, you can add some nicer bed sheets, pillows, and comforters. This will not only add glamor to your RV but also make your bed more comfortable to sleep in after a long day of activities. You could also acquire a velvet sleeping mattress or a lofty cot.

You can also add a rug to your bedroom, some reading material, slippers, and a table to make the room more comfortable and like home. In case you like to snooze during the day, you could acquire a hammock that could be essential for napping.

With your room, all glam and cozy, do not be surprised if you want to spend your whole day in the RV.

Control the Temperature

While traveling, there are times that you will experience some harsh weather. Just because you are having an adventure in the great outdoors, you do not have to endure the extreme cold or heat. There are campers with the notion that great camping entails putting up with harsh weather. However, glamping entails better camping and comfort as its main focus. If you cannot endure harsh weather, you could consider carrying a fan or heater on your trip. These will play a significant role in keeping your camping space comfortable.

In case there is electricity at your glamping site, you could carry a compact air conditioner or an evaporative cooler. These can be found on sites online. You need to be careful to keep your tent or camper airtight for it to be effective. There are also electric freestanding stove heaters that will provide heat in your space and make it much cozier. A retro-looking fan might also be a perfect option for a road trip.

Be Organized

Neatness can go a long way into glamping your space. To ensure that you do not have any clutter lying around, you can use wall hooks, organizers, bins, etc. They may not be glamorous, but they will enable the space to look better and more comfortable.

Pets

If you are considering living in an RV, you may be wondering how you are going to live with your pet(s) and travel with them from one place to another. Maybe that is even stopping you from traveling. But, you will be surprised at how well pets can adapt to an environment and live full time with you in an RV.

In fact, a lot of full-time RV owners live with their pets. Animals are the best at adjusting to conditions. They are not a barrier to RV life, although they could make the RV lifestyle a bit more complicated.

When it comes to living with pets in an RV, there are several factors that you need to consider. These factors include:

- Availability of space for the pets and the things they need

- The duration you are going to be on the road and how long you will take before stopovers.

- The distance of your journey

- The kind of animal you want to live with as well as its character

- Legal documents needed to live with the pet wherever you go

- The cost of living with the pet

With these factors in mind, you will be able to make an informed decision on whether you should go with your pet for the RV trip or not. If you decide to go on the trip with your pet. You have to be careful not to break any campsite rules or subject your pet to any sort of danger or problem.

For this reason, you have to do a few things to ensure the comfort of you, your pet, and those around you.

Planning the Ideal Itinerary

You need to plan a little more when it comes to traveling with your pet. Ensure that the destinations you go to are pet-friendly. These locations may include campgrounds, RV parks, as well as restaurants. It is awful to go to a spot only to discover that it is not pet-friendly.

To find good pet-friendly spots, you could check online on sites like GoPetFriendly.com, where thousands of pet-friendly establishments are listed. These places could be comfortable for you and your pet.

Packing the Appropriate Gear

Before you set out for your trip, take some time to make a list of everything you need to care for your pets. You could take about a week so that you can always add something new to the list whenever it comes up. This time is also ample enough to go shopping for your pet before the journey. This list will help you ensure that you do not forget anything important.

Note down the needs that may arise during your trip so that the next RV trip with your pet will be a lot easier.

Buckle Up

It is very dangerous to let your pet roam around when you are driving. An RV may feel like home, which may tempt you to let go of your pet. This is risky, not only for you but also for everyone else driving along the road you are on.

Driving an RV needs your full attention at all times. For this reason, your pets should always be in the same vehicle as you and buckled up. You can find carriers or a seat belt harness to ensure that they are well secured in the RV.

When you buckle up, you will keep your pet from distracting you while driving or being injured in case of an accident. The harnesses can be found anywhere at pet stores and online pet markets. With time, your pet will adapt to the harness and settle down every time you buckle it in place.

Be Aware of the Weather

Be sure to constantly keep an eye on the weather when traveling around with your pet. Look out for unstable temperatures, storms, or high winds.

Some RV campgrounds have storm shelters where you could take your pet in case of a storm. Locate them once you arrive at the campground and take your pet there in case of an emergency.

In case of heat, ensure that you take the necessary precautions. Always have a plan on how to protect your pet from adverse weather conditions.

Take Potty Breaks

When traveling with your pet, it is best to consider making time for more stopovers than you would when traveling without a pet. This is because your pet will need potty breaks a lot. Ensure that you also take walks in the park often and allow your dogs to enjoy the scent of the flowers. These breaks will also be good for you to take a rest and enjoy the environment. You can plan a hike somewhere and take your pet along with you. This will be a good experience for both you and your pet.

Be Considerate of Your Neighbors

More campgrounds and restaurants are becoming pet-friendly by the day and changing their policies. Most of these places allow entry with pets and also offer some pet services.

However, you should remember that taking your pets along with you to such places is a privilege. In case your pet is a nuisance to the people around you, you will be held accountable for its behavior. For this reason, ensure that you maintain good behavior in your pet and ensure that you respect the need for peace by other people.

Follow the pet rules and regulations. Keep it on a leash and ensure that barking is at a minimum. Also, and most importantly, always pick up your pet's waste. Do not leave your pet's poo lying around everywhere. Pick after your pet!

The greatest thing about RVing is having fun. Traveling with your pets should make this experience more fun for you as well as your pets. Traveling with them should be a time to kick back and have the best time with your best friends. This will make your trip more fun than you would ever think. Pets also need a little fun and outdoor experience. Traveling with them will also give them the most epic time of their lives.

Part 3: 101 RV Hacks

Food

As thrilling as it is to make your ideal home recipes on your trip, there are more amazing, novel, and exciting techniques of whipping up a savory meal when you are camping out in your RV. For instance, you can even use the sun's power to cook a meal. And no, not with solar panels, but the sun itself.

What you are capable of making in your rig actually depends more on the sort of RV you have. For example, cooking might be as it is at home while in a big Class A motorhome, which usually has a full-sized kitchen, a microwave, a stove, and an oven.

However, RVs are not designed alike. Therefore, below are several RV food hacks and skills that you may find useful during your journey.

Use a Campfire to Cook

This may seem like an obvious thing as it is common among a lot of people. There is a reason why it is a great idea. There is something enchanting about converting farm-fresh ingredients into a good, healthy meal above an uncovered fire. You will be surprised that this does not only work for s'mores and marshmallows, but also hot dogs, kebabs, bratwurst, and many other dishes.

Use an Instant Pot

This is an appliance that a lot of RVers swear by. It can do everything from pressure cooking to baking a cake in it. You can also sautee all in one tiny footprint that is RV-friendly. An instant pot is one of the greatest investments you can make in RV kitchen appliances.

Use a Solar Oven

Cooking using the power from the sun can be the best idea if you want to add an outdoorsy feel to your camping. A solar oven enables you to cook using the sun's power, and it hardly consumes any space in your RV.

If you are looking into boondocking and do not want to run the generator or cook over a smoky fire, then this is one excellent method of preparing a hot meal.

Use a Pizza Stone

If you miss having a pizza while outdoors, a pizza stone can be very helpful in preparing the snack you are craving for. Made of ceramic, this cooking equipment assures you of a crunchy, crusty base every time you use it. It can also be used for a number of other recipes like cookies and chicken fingers.

It is even more useful in RVs where it is placed beneath a gas oven, which is in most RVs. This helps distribute the heat equally. This means that every dish you make using will be better. It can also be used on top of a grill.

Unusual Storage Ideas

Here is a list of some of the ways that I used atypical items to enhance storage space in my tiny galley RV kitchen:

- Use an empty cereal box to store plastic wrap and aluminum foil boxes.

- Hang your hot pads on the inside of the kitchen cabinet doors with 3M hooks

- Use old pill bottles to store spices. Old cleaned out pill medicine bottles are smaller than mason jars and are easy to write on.

- Fill every nook and cranny. I kept a small basket in the microwave that was for chip bags and small wrapped snacks. When the microwave is not in use, it is just sitting empty.

Sleeping Hacks

Sleeping in an RV is not easy. Sometimes you have so much to do during your adventures from traveling, exploring, and working towards finishing projects that there is no time for sleep. You must have good rest unless you want to be tired and irritable in a place where you should be having fun.

So after struggling a bit with the discomfort of the RV bed and losing sleep, I did some research and found tips on getting better sleep in your RV.

Find a Secluded Spot

When you get to a campground, get a secluded spot away from neighbors and traffic. That can be a bit tricky, depending on the situation.

If you are in a packed campsite, request for the quietest spot available. Hosts understand their sites best and are able to place you at the most desirable spot. Additionally, ensure that you are away from the bathrooms. Waking up to the bathroom door slamming over and over at night can be such a nuisance.

Take it a step further and call the campground and make reservations for your campsite early enough and request for the quietest place available.

Turn off the lights at night

I have discovered that light contributes a lot to our sleep and wake cycle. Therefore, if you are a light sleeper like I am, you will sleep better with the lights off. To keep sunlight, parking lot lights, or headlights from cars from disturbing you at night and interrupting your sleep, we installed blackout curtains. You can also use blinds for the same purpose.

Some more light hacks include:

- Use solar stake lights to find your way to the RV.

- Add glow in the dark tape on your RV stairs to light your way up and down.

- If your dog needs to go out at night, put a glow necklace on him. That way, you can see where he is when he goes potty at night.

Acquire a Good Mattress

RV mattresses can be very uncomfortable. Therefore, acquiring a good mattress will be very helpful in getting you to have some good sleep. It is said that a good mattress will help keep you from neck and back issues. Therefore, the better mattress will not only glamp your RV space but also ensure that you are comfortable and free from a stiff neck or back that RV mattresses would give you.

Get Comfy Bedding

Pillows and bedsheets are essential when it comes to comfort in your RV. Ensure that you get a good pillow, whichever you may like. There are lumpy pillows and medium pillows that are both good for people with different tastes in pillows. Instead of carrying unused pillows from home, ensure that you get really good ones.

In addition, have the right bed sheets as they can add some comfort to your sleep at night. You can change the bedsheets often, depending on the weather. For winter, you can use a flannel whereas for summer you can use bed sheets that are cool and light. You will be surprised how much bed sheets can help you sleep better.

Limit Screentime

It can be enticing to start watching Netflix or scrolling down social media feeds at the end of the day to unwind. However, to get enough sleep while in our RVs, it is best to keep your screens and phones away.

I read somewhere that the light of a smartphone tricks our bodies into believing that it is daytime. The light causes our minds to want to stay awake and keep scrolling. This illustrates why it is harder to fall asleep or not get enough sleep because we are waking our bodies back up with the lights from the screen.

Zippered Bedding

These are normally used for kids, but can also be good for adults. This is because it makes it easier to make your bed in the morning. With zippered beddings, you will no longer struggle with a big comforter. It will even help save you some time in cramped living quarters.

Limit Caffeine

This may be hard for some people, but it is very beneficial. I struggled with staying away from caffeine in the evening, but eventually, I was able to stop drinking it. This resulted in better sleep at night. I believe it can work the same for you.

Sleeping Bags Lined with a Sheet

Sheet-lined sleeping bags are the trend these days. When you sew a flat sheet to fit well into a sleeping bag and add snaps to keep the sheet in place, you make a fine little sleeping place, which you can easily roll out every night and roll up every morning. The sheet renders a barrier between your body and the bag.

Stick to a Schedule

If you had a regular night time habit at home before RVing, then stick with it! Try your best to keep your routine even in your RV life on the road. You may not always manage to observe the schedule because of a lot of activities while camping.

Cleaning and Organizing Hacks

I love moving around without a struggle while living in an RV. Since living in an RV is meant to make life simple, it can also make things complicated when it comes to cleaning and organizing.

The following are hacks that will help you handle the issue of cleaning and organizing.

Decrease Your List of Cleaners

Keep your list of cleaning equipment to a minimum, with only the very necessary ones. This will help free up space for storage for other things like fun stuff.

Work Smart Not Hard

Give cleaning products some time to work. For instance, when cleaning the microwave, use some hot water to steam out the dirt.

Keep a bin for dirty shoes near the door to keep the floor clean. If the bin is outside the RV, put a lid on it.

Cleaning Entry Area

Take a moment every day to clean the indoor and outdoor entrance into your RV. It is important to clean your RV inside at the areas you first spot when you are at the entrance. This will also help you relax.

Take a Few Minutes a Day

You do not want to be cleaning your RV while on vacation. You want to spend the time enjoying the adventure. For this reason, cleaning your RV should not take much of your time.

If you take a few minutes every day to tidy up and organize things, the clutter will be kept under control and save you a lot of cleaning time and stress.

Be Organized

Have bins and storage baskets where you can put various things in. When you need to have storage under the bed or in cupboards, organized drawers where you can keep many things at one time is important.

Use Cleaning Tools that are Space Efficient

There is not very much room in an RV. For this reason, consider having multi-purpose tools like a canister vacuum, which is ideal for the RV. The vacuum can dust, vacuum, and fit easily in the compartments. In addition, it can be utilized for cleaning beach sand.

Acquire cleaning supplies that are multi-purpose. Lemon and baking soda are other excellent choices for all sorts of cleaning solutions. Using an all-purpose and natural cleaner is the best for a tight space.

Use Wet Wipes

A lot of wet wipes contain chemicals. However, they are very useful when it comes to cleaning your RV. They will save you loads of time when tidying up.

Air Freshness is Key

An air purifier is an excellent tool for maintaining fresh air inside your RV. I prefer the compact one, which I also use at home.

Use Organizers from Surprising Places.

You can use things like aluminum can tops and wood crates, which can work wonders in organizing some of your items in the RV, such as shoes and kitchen appliances.

Maintenance Hacks

You need to ensure that you maintain your RV well since it is your mobile home that you will constantly be moving around in. To ensure proper maintenance and upkeep of your RV, the following are a few hacks you could utilize.

Cover Up

A lot of RVers tend to forget the roof of the RV since they rarely get on top of the RV. For this reason, the roof is usually prone to damage from environmental factors like the sun. This can bring about a lot of problems and cost you big time. For this reason, it is important that you cover it up with the universal RV cover or an RV carport.

Also, don't forget to clean your awning gently with a soft scrub brush and a special cleaner. We use a cleaner that we picked up from Walmart, but there are lots of options on the market.

Generator Maintenance

Gasoline usually stays fresh for about thirty days. Therefore, it is a good idea to use your generator often and not allow it to sit idle for long. If you do, you would be forced to replace it as the gasoline may break down and cause damage to the generator. For great maintenance of the generator, you have to keep the gasoline flowing.

You can use the recommended way of running your generator for at least two hours every month. This will maintain its prime nature and keep it ready.

Check Things Out

A lot of RV owners deal with the issue of water dripping into the RV due to faulty seals, which normally deteriorate with time. Some brands notoriously use seals that are not great and wear out fast. When they wear out, they begin to allow water into the RV.

For this reason, it is important to constantly check your door and window seals to ensure that they are still intact and fit. Look around for water stains, cracks, and loose pieces that may allow water in.

Vent it Out

Heat usually damages a lot of things and causes them to deteriorate. Things that may be affected are seams, seals, flooring, as well as wall coverings. If not well maintained, heat may cause a lot of damage to them.

For this reason, keep your RV vents open so as to allow the proper flow of air in the vehicle as well as keep the temperature low. However, to keep yourself from the rain, ensure that you cover the exterior vents. Also, parking your RV in an area that is well covered will do wonders when it comes to your RV's lifespan.

Lubricate

To avoid the squeaky pop-out sound that can be produced from worn-out rails, you must lubricate them from time to time. The sound can be very irritating, like a nail on a chalkboard.

With proper lubrication, you will keep the rails from being corroded and rusty. Experts suggest that you apply some lubricant to your rails a couple of times per year, depending on how many times you use your RV. There are lubricant sprays made for slide-outs that cost about fifteen dollars. It is best to invest in it rather than incur the cost of replacing worn-out slide outs.

Tire Time

Keep your tires cleaned, covered, and protected when they are stationary. Ensure that they are not exposed to the sun as its rays swiftly depreciate the tires. They may need to be replaced due to rot and sun damage before they even wear out the tread.

There are UV protectants for tires such as 303 Aerospace Protectant. Cover your tires with an RV tire cover when storing your RV. Ensure that you also check the diameter of your wheels before acquiring them.

Keep Records

Keep a track record of the maintenance tasks that your RV has gone through. There are tools online such as "Maintain my RV" that can be helpful in tracking the maintenance history of your RV.

In the tools, you will have maintenance documents at a single place as well as get up-to-date reminders of due maintenance via email. It does not matter the sort of RV you have. A maintenance record is essential in ensuring constant proper maintenance.

If you're more of a paper person, you can get a maintenance logbook. I would suggest that you keep it in your RV and make detailed notes about your maintenance.

Fuel

Maintain proper weight on your RV to avoid excessive fuel consumption. Pack light and avoid carrying portable systems for water filtration instead of frequently topping off of freshwater tanks. Also, empty your holding tanks before leaving your location. For a lighter RV, you can also buy some camping materials related to your RV onsite rather than carrying them with you.

Lighting

Try out some off the grid camping so as to keep electrical usage low. Boondocking can be very helpful when it comes to saving electricity. You can also use low wattage LED lights, which give off clean and glowing light without wasting your solar reserves or battery.

You can also use a headlamp at night to do small activities in the RV, especially when you do not want to wake anyone from their sleep.

Also, RV LED lights are usually more pricey than traditional bulbs; however, they last longer and are more efficient when it comes to energy.

Staying Healthy

There are many ways you can maintain good health and keep fit while traveling in an RV.

Dieting

A lot of people find it difficult to diet while traveling. However, you can manage to diet with the right schedule and the right foods in your RV. Just like you keep fresh fruits and veggies at home, also can you keep them in your RV.

Despite the limited storage and no pantry or fruit bowl to keep your fruits, you can still have space to keep the fresh foods in your RV. Such places can include a multi-tier basket that can be quite handy in storing your fruits and veggies.

Shop Often

As a traveler, you have a lot of opportunities to visit farmers' markets and actual farms to shop for fresh foods. Since the multi-tier basket can hold a few fruits and veggies, going for shopping will keep you from snacking consistently on dry foods.

Local fresh produce straight from the farm is very healthy and will keep your carb and sugar intake low.

Pack a Picnic

This will aid in preventing you from having urgent stopovers at fast food joints and convenience stores. It will ensure that you maintain your healthy diet despite where you are.

Dine Out One Day

Eating out can be very tempting for a traveler since you are touring new areas with superb dining opportunities. Rather than keeping yourself from having any meal outings, allocate one day every week to go and dine out. Use this day to savor small eateries and get to enjoy the local food scene.

Hit the Gym

There are many campgrounds with gyms in them. Most are in RV resorts that have more amenities than the state parks. There, you can gain access to gyms, where you can do your workouts.

Get a Gym Membership

In case you desire a more focused exercise habit, you can join any gym chain. Most chains have locations in several states.

For these gyms, you may need to obtain a membership that will help you access that particular chain of gyms in any state where you travel.

From the gyms, you will get childcare in case you have kids, as well as showers that you can use when boondocking.

Be Active

These can include hiking, canoeing, rock climbing, and swimming among the many entertaining activities you have access to when camping. When you miss your time at the gym or simply want to have fun doing something else, you can try going for activities that will also help keep your body fit.

Plan Meals

Come up with a schedule for meals throughout the entire week. Ensure that these meals are healthy and that it is possible for you to cook them. You can use the instant pot, which will really help you cook a lot of meals in an RV.

Travel Slowly

As unrelated as it is to fitness, this hack will actually help a lot. When you have too many things scheduled for too little time, you are prone to forget about dieting and keeping fit. Therefore, slow your pace down and allocate proper time for activities that you want to do in a day, including times for meals and workouts.

Water, Water, Water

Yes, water is life. Since traveling entails a lot of activity, you are prone to becoming dehydrated over time. For this reason, have a water bottle that you can carry around and drink water from whenever you are outdoors. Keep yourself hydrated.

Money

Although traveling is the main purpose of your journey, there are activities that you will need to do to make sure that you do not stay broke. Therefore, there are several activities that you can do that can help you earn some money as well as save money.

Saving Money

First, let us look at how you can save the money that you already have.

Travel Seasonally

When you travel in seasons, you will be able to manage expenses accrued from weather-related issues. For instance, if you travel at times when it is neither too cold nor too hot, you will manage to save on the number of times you use electricity and the generator, which may consume a lot of propane.

Boondock

Boondocking will really help you save some cash since you are not using any electricity, water, or sewer hookups that would otherwise consume a lot. This is also more peaceful and enjoyable. Boondocking means to camp primitively, usually on free sites such as BLM (Bureau of Land Management) land.

Cook More

It is very tempting for a traveler to dine out every day. Everyone loves a new dish in a new area at some point. However, doing so will consume much of your money. For this reason, prepare your own and also pack food when going for outings like hikes.

Join RV Clubs

When in a club, you will be required to pay some amount of fees. However, you can save a lot from being a member of a club because you may get amenities at some campgrounds for a cheaper cost or absolutely free.

Making Money

To make money, you can:

Work Online

There are many jobs that you can do online, including having your own website where you talk about different issues. There are many people online willing to pay others to do their activities. Get browsing and find job opportunities.

Try Workamping

There are many jobs that you can find in the area where you are living. You can be a gym instructor or a data entry clerk at a company in the area. There are many jobs that you can do for a few hours a day and get paid. All you need to do is ask around.

There are a number of campgrounds that hire campers to work with them in exchange for either pay or a free stay at the campgrounds. Ask ahead when making reservations if they are hiring workampers. You may have to clean the bathrooms, do routine maintenance, or keep up the grounds.

This can not only earn you money but also help you live on the campground for absolutely free. You can spend your idle time doing jobs around the campground and earn your living.

Find Local Jobs

Most campgrounds have boards where they make announcements on an occasional basis. You can have a look at the board and find jobs advertised there like receptionist job, bartender, etc. You can work at any that you find suitable.

Sell Your Services

In case you have been in a certain area for a while, you can offer to be a tour guide to other new campers at the campgrounds. You can also offer to clean RVs or do some chores for a fee.

Sell Stuff

You can start your own business that you can do wherever you go. Get a product, make a product, market it, sell it, and make a living.

Be a Blogger

Many full-time nomads or RVers find that becoming an online influencer can net a tidy profit. You can write blogs, make vlogs (YouTube videos), self-publish a book, and even become big on Instagram and make revenue from these ventures, just telling your story of your unique life. Companies, especially outdoor and RV-centered companies, might send you free products in exchange for a post or video about the product. Often times, you can earn a commission from affiliate marketing – meaning that if someone clicks on a special link and makes a purchase, you get a portion of that sale.

Navigation

RVs, as I mentioned earlier, are not like the usual cars that we drive. They need some level of prowess to maneuver. Below are a few navigation tips and tricks.

Practice

It has been said that "practice makes perfect." Well, this is the case for RVs as well. Before you set out for your journey, it is important that you practice well and be conversant with the RV. Focus on key issues such as parking and turning, among many other maneuvers.

Observe the Weather

No driver wants surprises. For this reason, check out the weather carefully and prepare for it. You can monitor the weather by downloading apps that will help you know the weather in a certain region, as well as any likelihood of changes in the weather.

Adjust Your Mirrors

It can be tricky to see what is behind you while driving an RV. However, it is necessary that you are constantly aware of the vehicles driving behind you all the time. Therefore, take your time to properly adjust your mirrors before you set out on your journey. This will ensure safety while on the road.

Don't Drive Tired

It is easy to get tired when driving an RV. It is not the easiest of vehicles to drive. So, when you get tired, pull over somewhere safe and take a rest; otherwise, you will endanger your life and the lives of those on the road with you.

Go Slow

Do not be in a hurry as high speed can cause a lot of damage to the RV, and a lot of harm to other people around you. For the sake of safety on the road, ensure that you maintain the right speed.

Observe Courtesy

Be courteous on the road. Do not be a road-hog, no matter how large your vehicle may be. Keep in mind that other people also have a right to be on the road just like you.Use your signals whenever you make a turn and respect other drivers on the road.

Tail Swing is Everything

With the proper knowledge of your tail swing, you will manage to pack your rig without causing any damage to your RV or anyone's property. You can get an understanding of this during practice. You could ask someone for help in helping you understand the tail swing. The person can help you measure the tail swing as well as guide you when packing.

Avoid Tailgating

Keep your distance from other vehicles around you. You do not want to hit another driver's vehicle while on the road. The best distance is about 400-500 feet from the other vehicle. This will help reduce the chances of accidents.

Braking Habits

When it comes to braking, RVs are not like typical cars. Due to the weight of the RV, you will need to properly plan yourself before you can apply the brake. Ensure that you do not have to brake suddenly. Looking ahead, thinking ahead, and paying attention are the keys to saving lives!

Far Right

Stay on the far right. This is a rule of thumb in driving. However, an RV driver should ensure that he or she stays in the far right lane due to the size of the RV. You can only leave far right when you need to make an exit from the main road or are passing a much slower vehicle. Make it a habit to travel in the far right lane.

Safety

First Aid

Anything could occur while on the road. For proper preparation for emergencies, ensure that you have a first aid kit packed with all the necessities. A first aid kit can be purchased pre-stocked, or you can create your own.

A good first aid kit should have:

- Band-Aids in several sizes

- Gauze pads

- Antiseptic wipes (like alcohol pads)

- Burn ointment

- Antibiotic ointment (like Neosporin)

- Rubber gloves

- Anti-itch cream for bug bites

- Epi-pen or snake bite kit

Be Defensive

Not everyone you meet on the road means you well. There are always evil people ready to take advantage of people and cause them harm. For this reason, it is good to have a few things that you can use for self-defense. Among those things is pepper spray, which is good since it is easily portable.

Have a Plan

Prepare your RV in case of an emergency. For instance, my husband and I have a place in our RV, which is designated only for emergencies. In case anything happens, we will have a place to exit the RV from. Discuss where you will meet outside if there is an emergency. Have a place to meet up and take a headcount, especially if you need to evacuate pets or children, too.

An emergency might not just occur while you're inside your RV; you might encounter unexpected events while adventuring about. Here are some more general safety tips and tricks.

Travel in Groups

There is safety in numbers. When you are many, chances of a bad occurrence are less guaranteed, unlike when you travel alone. Also, you will be able to get assistance in case anything happens.

Carry a Smartphone

You need to be able to call 911 or someone in case of any emergency. It is, therefore, very important that you have your phone with you while on the road.

Switch Off the Generator

Do not leave the generator on when sleeping at night as it generates carbon monoxide that is harmful and could possibly lead to death.

Do Safety Checks

Ensure that your vehicle is well-set for travel. Look out for leaks, cords, or hose connected to sewers, mirror positions, and many other aspects of safety. This will help you ensure that your vehicle is in the right condition for travel.

Have a Dog

Dogs can help alert you of anything that is coming. They are, therefore, good for alerting the owner of danger. Dogs are also protective of their owners, and they will try to protect you whichever way they can when harm comes your way. They are indeed man's best friend!

Be Diligent

Yes, always be alert and ready for anything. Keep in mind that anything can happen during your journey. You do not want to be caught off-guard. Be observant of your surroundings, know where you are, and know-how to get help if the need arises.

One way to keep track of where you are when you travel frequently is to hang a small whiteboard on the inside of one of your kitchen cabinets. Write down emergency contact numbers for the locality and take note of your campground address and which site you're at. When your address changes all the time, it can be easy to forget where you are!

Comfort Hacks

These are hacks to ensure that your journey is as comfortable as ever.

Prepare Early

Ensure that you take enough time to prepare for your journey. This will help you not to forget key things that you need to keep your journey comfortable. Imagine in your mind what your typical day from top to bottom will look like while on your journey. Try to account for all aspects of your day from sleeping, eating, hygiene, and recreation. Think about how to make your day easier and more manageable.

Use Folder Boxes

These can help you in storage, especially kitchenware. When your kitchen stuff is kept in an organized manner, you will be able to comfortably access them and keep the RV organized.

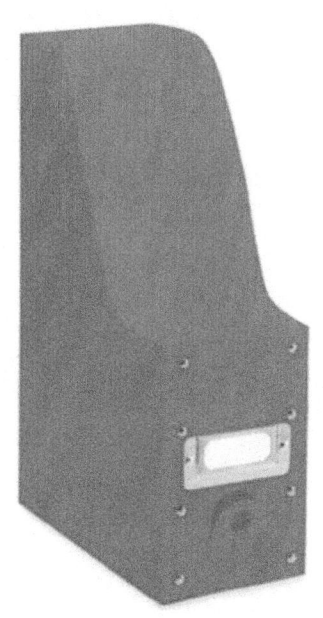

Install Push Lights

Poor lighting can make your journey very uncomfortable. For this reason, ensure that you install good lighting with push lights in cabinets or corners to provide a bit of light in those areas.

It will also help with keeping overnight lighting to a minimum, as most push lights are dimmer and run on batteries that won't drain the generator lights or disturb your sleep mates.

Get Hooked

Hooks can be used to hang things like towels, clothes, and hats. You can acquire double hooks that can hold more items than single hooks. These hooks will prevent things from falling around the RV.

Get Cushioned

Invest in a vent cushion. It is hard to regulate the temperature in an RV since most of them are not ventilated. For this reason, a vent cushion will be very helpful as it will help regulate the temperature in the RV during hot or cold seasons.

Get What You Pay For

Utilize the amenities at the campgrounds. The resources at the campgrounds are there for you to use. You paid for the use of them already! For this reason, it is good to make good use of them to ensure that your life in an RV is as comfortable as it can be.

Be Creative

Get creative with your space. With neatness and a bit of creativity, you can maximize the space that you have in your RV. You can utilize unexpected things like cleaned out soups cans to store things that would otherwise take up too much space.

Hanging Storage Everywhere

Acquire toiletry pockets (hanging toiletry bags). These will help you keep your toiletry well arranged so you will be able to find them easily. When all your toiletries are scattered all over, you will have a challenging time finding them and waste a lot of time. With toiletry pockets, however, you will be able to easily access all your toiletries whenever you need them.

Regulate Windows

Install reflectix on your windows. These can be found in home improvement stores around your area. They can make your RV comfortable by regulating the temperature of your RV.

Recreation Hacks

Here is a list of ways to have fun while nomading:

- Carry DVDs with music and movies that you can listen to or watch during your stay in the RV.

- Make friends during your journey. These friends could be found at campgrounds or events. Ensure that you meet a friend or two.

- Use a map. Go old school and use a paper map. Forget the GPS and play a map game where you try to physically find a location that is on the map.

- Attend events. This is where you will meet lots of people as well as learn a lot.

- Go out for dinners. There is nothing as good as treating your taste buds to a new savory dish that you probably never tasted before. Go out on a foodie adventure.

- Have some booze. Alcohol always has a way of making everything fun (for a while). Pack a six-pack or two and sip them around the campfire.

- Play games. Tabletop and card games can add some fun to your stay in the RV.

- Take photos of your adventure. Make memories by taking photos of the places you go to. You can make the moments more fun by sharing them with your friends on social media.

- Go for hikes. These are healthy and fun at the same time. You will get to explore the area as well as keep fit from all the hiking.

- Share. Yes, sharing can be fun. You can make a nice dish and invite your neighbors over for dinner or even hold a low-key party at your campsite. Create your own fun!

Conclusion

As you already can already see by now, the RV life is not as complicated as some may assume. In fact, it is more fun, and you can achieve much more while on the journey.

There are various RVs that you could purchase or even rent and go on a trip. You can take your family with you on vacation, even your pets, and experience a grand lifestyle. It feels good to explore the country as it has so much to offer and so much to teach.

Go out and marvel in the beauty of nature and link up with people who have similar passions as you do. Believe me. You will enjoy your journey and life in an RV

Do not be afraid. Set out and explore the beauty of your country!

Made in the USA
Middletown, DE
08 November 2020